THE EXCEPTIONAL VERA GOOD

THE EXCEPTIONAL VERA GOOD

A LIFE BEYOND THE POLKA DOT DOOR

NANCY SILCOX

WIPF & STOCK · Eugene, Oregon

CMU PRESS

2017

THE EXCEPTIONAL VERA GOOD

Wipf & Stock
An imprint of Wipf and Stock Publishers
199 W. 8th Avenue, Suite 3
Eugene OR, 97401
www.wipfandstock.com

CMU Press
500 Shaftesbury Blvd
Winnipeg, Manitoba
R3P 2N2

PAPERBACK ISBN : 978-1-5362-5929-4
HARDCOVER ISBN: 978-1-5362-5930-0

Cover: A photograph of Dr. Vera Good overlays an image of the set of "Polka Dot Door," a TVO educational children's television program that ran from 1971 to 1993.
Portrait photo courtesy of Nancy Silcox.
TVO "Polka Dot Door" images courtesy of Travis Doucette / www.rebelbox-media.com

Cover and interior design: Matt Veith

Library and Archives Canada Cataloguing in Publication

Silcox, Nancy, 1949-, author
    The exceptional Vera Good : a life beyond the Polka dot door
/ Nancy Silcox.

Includes bibliographical references.
ISBN 978-1-987986-03-7 (softcover)

    1. Good, Vera, 1915-. 2. Television producers and directors--Canada--Biography. 3. Educators--Canada--Biography.
4. Mennonites--Canada--Biography. 5. Biographies. I. Title.

PN1992.4.G66A3 2017   791.45092   C2017-907013-4

When you want to teach children to think, you begin by treating them seriously when they are little, giving them responsibilities, talking to them candidly, providing privacy and solitude for them, and making them readers and thinkers of significant thoughts from the beginning. That's if you want to teach them to think.

BERTRAND RUSSELL

TABLE OF CONTENTS

Preface

Early winter of 2016 saw me casting about for a substantial writing project that I could sink my teeth into. Magazine writing had kept me occupied since the winding down of my previous book, *Famous Canadians and the Pets They Love*, for the Ontario Veterinary College in 2015. And, if truth be known, I was at loose ends.

Soliciting nominations for worthy subjects from friends and family invariably brought no reward but instead an incredulous "You're writing another book? The ink is hardly dry on the last one!" Seeking a wider audience to canvas, I turned to Facebook and posted the notification: "Wanted: biography subject, with a compelling story to tell; male or female."

Within minutes I had responses – dozens at least. The suggestions ran the gamut from successful politicians, businessmen, and women, to writers, artists, and athletes. A worthy group, but not anyone to light my spark. My earlier biographies, *Edna's Circle: Edna Staebler's Century of Friendships* on the late writer and *Food That Really Schmecks* cookbook maven, and *Midwife Elsie Cressman: A Purposeful Life*, had set a high standard.

Disappointed, I vowed to check Facebook one last

time before moving on. And there it was, from historian and writer Marion Roes of Waterloo. "Vera Good has had an interesting life," posted Marion. "I'd nominate her."

A light glimmered on my darkened computer screen.

I had met Vera in 2007 when her family's foundation, the Milton R. Good Foundation, Inc., had funded *Edna's Circle*. At the time of that publication, Vera, then ninety-two, was living at Chartwell Terrace on the Square, the upscale assisted-living suites in Waterloo, Ontario.

I paid a visit to Vera to thank her for her family's generosity and learned bits and pieces of her life story, including what she called her "main claim to fame" as the creator and Executive Producer of TVOntario's long-running children's series *Polka Dot Door*. During our conversation I also gleaned that she had founded one of Ontario's first programs for gifted children at the Etobicoke School Board. She had the distinction of being Ontario's first woman Inspector of Schools in the early 1960s. And she held a Doctorate in Education from Columbia University in New York City. I had also learned that Vera's background was of Old Order

Mennonite stock. Finding this variable at odds with her academic achievements, I sensed that indeed there was a rich story to be told.

Thanking Marion Roes for her worthy suggestion, I was committed to tracking Vera down. "I'm fairly sure she is still living," I suggested to my husband, Louis, "but she has to be close to 100." I wondered if she remained cognitively sharp and, more crucial to book writing, if she had the endurance for many weeks of interviews.

A later visit to Vera answered my questions. Now living at Norview Lodge Long-Term Residence Facility in Simcoe, she had slowed down physically but her faculties remained sharp, and her enthusiasm to go on the journey that I was proposing keen. And so in late March of 2016, Dr. Vera Good and I set out on a year-long collaboration.

And what a singular year it was.

Born in 1915, only one year into Canada's involvement in the World War I, Vera led me through historical events that touched her life: the Great Depression, World War II, the assassination of Mohandas Gandhi and the birth of India as an independent nation; the movement for women's rights; the dawn of the age of technology and the emergence of the media as a pivotal social force.

Along the way, Vera's story also touched on intensely personal matters: finding love and losing it; self-questioning, then re-affirmation of abilities; discrimination in the workplace; loneliness, joy of family; disability and loss of independence in old age.

Over the course of fifty weekly interviews, Vera and I came to know – and trust each other – well. Entering her 102nd year, Dr. Vera Good remained the essence of the youthful Vera: intellectually curious, cognitively astute, introspective, and self-aware – with an admirable sense of personal strengths and failings.

Having attained high professional success both in education and media, she counts as her most cherished personal memories her years growing up on a Waterloo farm, surrounded by a loving family and an enduring faith.

A loving thank you, Dr. Vera Mary Good, for filling my own cup with your presence.

New Hamburg
April 2017

Acknowledgements

This labour of love could not have seen fruition without the assistance of a large cast of players – many of whom pointed me in the correct direction to uncover Waterloo County and Woolwich Township history. Others led me through the volumes of Ministry of Education and the archives of TVOntario.

I would be remiss if I did not especially thank James Good and the Good Foundation, Inc., for allowing this book to see the light of day and with it the life story of the remarkable Dr. Vera Good.

Thanks go as well to the following individuals:

A special thank you to Darryl Bonk, the "guardian" of the invaluable website Waterloo Region Generations. To Joan and Paul Good, Marybeth Smith, and Laureen Harder-Gissing, keeper of the Mennonite Archives of Ontario at Conrad Grebel University College at the University of Waterloo; Marjorie Rosekat and Howard Parliament; Michael Harris, MPP for Kitchener-Conestoga, and Office Manager Rob Willett; Robyn Hall and Babs Church, TVO; Ontario Ministry of Education May Nazar and Anne-Marie Flanagan; MCC Canada Executive Director Rick Cober Bauman, Joline Patfield and Frank Peachy of MCC Akron, PA;

Maebelle Knechtel Bell, Ernie Ritz, Louis Silcox, Mabel Hunsberger, Dr. Carol Duncan, Marion Roes, Joyce Stankiewicz, Elaine Gross, Dennis Willms, Barbara Draper, Rev. Maurice Martin, Sam Steiner, Dr. Paul Tiessen, Dan Shenk, Marilyn and Peter Etril Snyder, Greg McKinnon of the Toronto District School Board, Elizabeth King, and Dr. Marlene Epp.

And finally, my partners at Strong Start Waterloo Region: Machelle Denison and Christina Proctor.

PART ONE

Of the Old Order Community

1

Deep Roots, Strong Faith

As a centenarian, Dr. Vera Good's personal memories stretch back to those dark days after the end of the Great War. They gain substance as the tumultuous Roaring Twenties blend into the Great Depression. Memories of family dominate, giving insight into Mennonite life in the early years of the twentieth century. For where Vera was born and raised, in rural Waterloo County, the Mennonite "way" proliferated ... and prospered.

At the turn of the twentieth century, Waterloo and northwestern Wellington counties were largely undeveloped, with only small farms dotting the rolling landscape. But given the richness of the soil and the work ethic of the settlers who had populated the area, Waterloo region would steadily grow and prosper. The majority of the farmers were descendants of Pennsylvania Mennonites who had immigrated to Waterloo County in the early 1800s.

Near the end of the nineteenth century, philosophical divisions within the Mennonite Church had
led to splinter groups forming in four geographic areas
of northeastern North America: Indiana and Ohio;
Lancaster County, Pennsylvania; Rockingham County,
Virginia; and Waterloo County in the province of
Ontario.[1] Those electing to remain of the "Old Order"
(sometimes called Wisler Mennonites), whose adher-
ents eschewed innovations such as Sunday School and
evangelical Sunday evening meetings, joined together
"in brotherhood" in 1889. In Ontario, the Old Orders
were led by Bishop Abraham W. Martin of St. Jacobs, a
community north of Waterloo Township.[2]

One of the most prosperous and respected of the
Waterloo Old Order Mennonites was Isaac D. Martin.[3] Isaac was born in Waterloo Township in 1844,
five generations after his forbear David Martin had left
Switzerland in 1727 to settle in Lancaster County. In
1865, Isaac married Esther Bauman. They first resided
on a farm north of Floradale, Ontario, and there the
first four of the couple's seven children were born. Mary,
the youngest of the seven and Vera Good's mother, was
born on November 13, 1883. As Isaac's fortunes and
family size increased, the Martins relocated: first to a

property east of Elmira, then to a farm on the north shore of the Conestoga River, east of the hamlet of Hawkesville.

Within the Old Order tradition, higher education played virtually no role. Building parochial schools to educate Mennonite children of the community took second place to barn, house, and church construction. Still, most Old Order parents saw the value of literacy. They sent their children to the local public school up until they completed grade 8 or turned fourteen. At that point, Ontario law allowed children to leave school for the work world. For Old Order girls, that work was assisting with housework and caring for younger siblings; boys spent their days helping in the barn or in the field. Most girls, after their mandatory time working at home, would seek factory jobs. In Waterloo County, Kitchener (called Berlin until 1916) was a thriving factory town with jobs a-plenty in the textile, leather, steel, and rubber industries.

Isaac and Esther Martin were no different from other parents in the community, and each of their seven children left school when they turned fourteen. It is in Isaac where the anomaly presents itself. A progressive and intelligent man with political sensitivities, Isaac saw the value of having an Old Order voice on the local school board. Apparently the community agreed, and the highly respected Isaac was elected a trustee to the Elmira Public School Board. Records of the December 31, 1879 annual meeting of the S.S. #4 Woolwich, Elmira School Board indicate "Isaac Martin to be elected Trustee for the next three years. Carried."[4] Isaac served in this capacity for a number of years past his initial election.

Isaac's granddaughter Vera Good comments on her relative's unusual footnote in education history. "I doubt if there was another Old Order Mennonite in Ontario sitting on a public school board. Grandfather Isaac was a man ahead of his time."[5] Waterloo Region historian Ernie Ritz agrees: "I'm not aware of any other Old Order in Waterloo ... serving in this capacity."[6]

Mary, Isaac and Esther's youngest child, was, like her father, an intelligent and outgoing individual. She surely regretted leaving school at age fourteen. Still, the Old Order tradition must be followed, and she would remain at home for at least a year, assisting her mother with housework and other farm responsibilities. After this interval, she might "work out" as a housekeeper or babysitter for neighbours.

Tragedy came knocking on the Martin door in 1900, when Mary was eighteen: Esther died during a typhoid fever epidemic. With her older siblings now married or "working out," Mary, still living at home, moved into the role of full-time housekeeper for her father. Did the sociable Mary Martin chafe at such heavy responsibilities, as she surely had when she left school? Or did the dutiful teenager fulfill them without question? Vera speculates that given her mother's character, there were moments of both. The fact that she was baptized into the Old Order Church in 1902, at age nineteen, also suggests her mature, responsible character.

But Mary would not remain in her father's house for long. Fate would soon bring a handsome twenty-eight-year-old farm labourer named Henry Good into her life.

2
The Goods

Born to Menno and Johanna Good on October 17, 1877, Henry was the seventh generation of a family of three Mennonite brothers who had emigrated from Switzerland to America in 1737.[7] Abraham, Christian, and Peter Good first arrived in Philadelphia, then moved on to Lancaster County in Pennsylvania, where a large number of Mennonites had settled. Records show that Abraham died six years after arrival and left no heirs. Peter eventually moved to Virginia and married, but no information about his successors remains. The family line, which extended to Henry Good, traces its lineage to the middle brother, Christian.

It seemed that location as much as hard work and thriftiness determined financial success with respect to farming in these early, Victorian days. In the case of Menno Good, Henry's father, location was all. Menno and Johanna Good had settled in the area known as the Sandhills near the Elora "swamp," south of the hamlet of Salem and northwest of present-day Guelph. The land's yield was poor, and the Good family struggled to make ends meet. It was unlikely that any of the eight Good offspring, including Henry, the sixth born, would inherit a successful farm operation.

After his schooling ended, Henry "worked out" at various neighbouring farms. When he couldn't find employment close to home, Henry travelled farther afield. He is known to have worked as a farmhand as far away as Plattsville in Oxford County, even hiring out to farms in German Mills, in the present-day municipality of Markham.

While Vera hesitates to call her father a rebel, she does admit that he followed the road less travelled as far as religious faith is concerned. Raised as an Old Order, Henry hadn't followed the usual route to church membership. Most youth joined the church by the time they were in their mid to late teens. Henry had deferred. The reasons for this remain clouded; however, Vera speculates that "perhaps Dad had philosophical reasons. He might have had issues with the severity of the Old Order. He was, after all, a very shy and retiring man. Or perhaps the distant locations where he found work prevented him from joining the local church."

In any case, when Henry Good's eye was taken by young Mary Martin, youngest daughter of the respected Old Order pillar Isaac D., he had not taken out any church membership.

3

Henry and Mary

Vera believes that her parents may have become acquainted at a meetinghouse (church) social get-together, likely at the Martin Meetinghouse north of the present-day city of Waterloo.[8] This building served as the house of worship for Old Order Mennonite families in the area. "Church was the link that bound most Mennonites together," Vera states. But the place of the meeting of baptized and church-going Mary Martin and Henry Good, a non-attender, raises some questions. Was Henry rethinking his anti-church standard? Or perhaps he had been in attendance at the church function on the invitation of a friend? Perchance Henry, now in his mid-twenties, had begun to search for a wife?

Whatever the case, it appears that the match was an agreeable one. In time, Henry Good asked Isaac D. Martin for the hand of his youngest daughter, Mary, in marriage. Given Henry's renegade status in the Old Order community, it seems surprising, at first glance, that Isaac gave his blessing. On second thought, given Isaac D.'s own rarefied role as an Old Order school trustee, his agreement may be less puzzling.

A photo of the young Mary Martin gives insight into Mary's character as well. An attractive and confident-looking young woman stares directly at the camera. While she is wearing a proper high-necked, modest garment acceptable to the Old Order faith, the material and design are anything but austere. A satin bow and oval-jewelled brooch at the neckline, with carved buttons fastening the dress together and a flower corsage at the young woman's breast, are typical turn-of-the-century Victorian fashion.

With no date or reference to the time of the photo, one can only speculate that Mary is in her late teens at the time of the sitting and not yet baptized into the Old Order Church. Rick Cober Bauman, Executive Director of MCC Canada, whose lineage is Old Order, comments: "My own grandmother's photo taken before she was baptized shows her wearing quite fancy dress, including jewellery."[9] Cober Bauman proposes that for some teenage girls, "gussying up" for a formal portrait was a rite of passage before they were baptized, an observation others have also made.[10] Given that Mary's baptism took place in 1902, this speculation rings true. Another possibility is that the photo was taken after 1902, and Mary had left the Old Order Church. It is possible that by the time of her betrothal to Henry

Good, she was adhering to the more moderate Mennonite Conference ways.

Questions notwithstanding, the wedding of Mary
Martin and Henry Good was set for December 26,
1905. The place of the ceremony would be the bride's
home. And the officiating pastor? Records indicate that
the wedding of Henry Good, of no fixed church membership, and Mary Martin, of Old Order Mennonite,
was performed by Mennonite Conference Bishop Jonas
Snyder (Snider).[11] A search into the esteemed church-
man's credentials may assist in explaining the choice.

Born in Waterloo County, Jonas was the son of
Waterloo mill owner and Mennonite minister Elias
Snyder. The elder Snyder pastored the David Eby Congregation (later renamed Waterloo Mennonite Church,
and today Erb Street Mennonite Church) in Waterloo.[12] During the "modern vs. traditional" schism that
rocked the Mennonite Church in 1889, Elias sided with
the Old Order while son Jonas threw his lot toward
the future.[13] In 1892, Jonas was ordained as minister of
the David Eby Congregation, which Elias had vacated
during the schism. In 1895 Jonas was named Bishop
for Waterloo Township. History reflects Bishop Jonas
Snyder's reputation as a conciliatory church official who
preached in English, sanctioned Sunday School for
children and Sunday evening church social evenings. In
a bold move, he also sanctioned an all-female church
committee.

Vera offers her thoughts on why Mennonite

Conference Bishop Snyder may have agreed to officiate at her parents' wedding, held in the home of staunch Old Order pillar Isaac D. Martin: "The Bishop agreed in recognition of my grandfather Isaac's high standing in the community." Waterloo historian Barbara Draper points to another possible factor: "The Old Order split had only happened fifteen years before; many families straddled the split at the time."[14] One can only speculate on the reaction of the less progressive of Mary's Old Order relations to the wedding ceremony – and the participants. Continuing down the road less travelled he had embarked on as an Old Order school trustee, Isaac Good must surely have cemented his reputation as a man of conciliation with his youngest daughter's wedding.

4

Starting Out

For the first several years after their marriage, Henry and Mary lived with Isaac on the Martin farm. Viola, the couple's first child, was born there on June 13, 1907. This arrangement allowed Mary to continue to keep house for her father while she and Henry looked for affordable housing of their own. Whether Henry continued to hire out to neighbouring farms or ran his father-in-law's operation is unknown.

When a three-acre plot of land on Bearinger Road in north Waterloo Township came onto the market in 1909, Henry purchased it. A resourceful and hard-working man, a jack of many trades and master of none, he began construction on a six-room, two-storeyed double-brick house. Lacking finances to hire help, Henry built the home primarily on his own. Only one photo survives of Henry and Mary Good's home, but what appears there indicates Henry's skill as a bricklayer and woodworker. The house features quoined corners of the brick face of the house; a side view shows Mary's beloved porch.

While Henry saw to the details of exterior construction, Mary focused on aesthetics. "Mother liked good things, and there were certain things that she definitely wanted for a house of her own," says Vera. "Good things" included a gracious veranda, which faced the road side of the house. Inside was a formal centre hall and a large living room; dining-room picture windows gave the house, not yet wired for electricity, light. Stairs to the upper floor were of rich cherry wood, with a matching wood newel post and banister.

With another daughter, Lorene, born on July 21, 1909, Mary and Henry were on their way to filling the three upper bedrooms. After the completion of the house, Henry began work on a two-storey "bank barn." "Animals on the ground floor, hay and straw upstairs," says Vera. At three acres, the Henry Good property wasn't large enough to grow wheat or corn to sell on the market, or to feed a large herd. It was sufficient to provide food for the Good's modest menagerie, which included several milking cows, two horses, pigs, chickens, and ducks.

Around the time of the Good family's move to their Waterloo north property, they took up formal church membership. Records at Erb Street Mennonite Church – then Waterloo Mennonite Church – indicate that in 1910, "Henry and Mary Good, their daughter Viola, age 2¾ and daughter Lorene, age ½ year" were included on a list of new church members.[15] The historical entry prompts some questions. Now married five years and the parents of two daughters, why did Henry and Mary Good delay joining a new church until now? Had Mary attended church in her home community until their relocation to north Waterloo? We can assume that up until 1910, Henry remained without church membership. Vera reflects on the matter:

> *I doubt if Mother and Father attended any church regularly before they joined Erb Street Mennonite. Mother would have been too busy raising two daughters and moving into a new house. So she probably didn't have time. And church for Father hadn't been part of his life for years, so he wouldn't have felt a pressure to attend Sunday services.*

Whatever the rationale, by 1910, with two children born and another on the way, the Henry Goods decided it was nigh on time to become part of a church community. Vera has vivid memories of walking south along the railway tracks that cut through the rapidly growing town of Waterloo to Waterloo Mennonite Church – a distance of three kilometres each way – in Sunday-go-to-meeting clothes. "Given that the tracks were always cleared for the trains, it was the fastest way to get to church."

5

A Happy Home Life

Every two years or so, Henry and Mary Good's family grew. Viola and Lorene were followed by Milton on June 20, 1911; Edna on May 26, 1913; Vera on November 13, 1915; Erma on March 8, 1917; Robert on January 4, 1924; and Harold on October 15, 1926. The family mourned the loss of two stillborn babies.

Looking back on her parents' relationship and marriage, Vera points to their different personalities:

> *I'd call my parents' marriage a happy one, but one which had two people of very different temperaments coming together. Dad was not just a bit quiet and shy, he was painfully shy. Grandma Good told us that when he was a boy and the family would have company, he would hide under the bed till everyone was gone!*

On the other hand, Mary Good loved company

and fellowship. Vera believes that these two dispositions must have collided from time to time. An early photo bears out Vera's assessment of her parents' personalities. In the formal portrait, Henry, mouth drawn tight and hands clenched on his lap, sits uncomfortably attired in the requisite Edwardian high-neck collar, bow tie, and woollen suit. A relaxed Mary by his side smiles with both her mouth and her eyes. This is clearly a woman of confidence.

Although personalities differed, core values did not. On the importance of family, surely the couple faced each day as a unit. While Henry was a conscientious provider for his growing brood, Mary Good was a marvel at organization. "Mother somehow made time for each of us," reports Vera. Even better, this mother had imagination. "I remember her cleaning out an old smokehouse that had been used once to butcher hogs. She aired out the building, scrubbed the floor, and papered the walls. It made a perfect place for us to play dolls." Vera fondly remembers her mother being an occasional guest at their tea parties: "And she always brought cookies." The Good children also prized time with their father. The memory of standing with her older sister Edna on Henry's big rubber boots, still on his feet, as he shuffled across the kitchen floor brings a warm smile to Vera's face.

No matter his good intentions, finding a steady source of income to feed his large family was a challenge for Henry Good. Vera offers this insight: "Dad was a hard worker, but he wasn't a skilled worker. The garden and our farm animals kept us from going hungry, but it wasn't enough to support a family of ten." So Henry Good relied on various entrepreneurial ventures to fill the financial void. An early business saw the Goods selling produce grown in the garden at the local farmers' market. The next, a more complicated venture, was a milk delivery route.

> *It was a two-day process. On the first day, Father collected raw (unpasteurized) milk from farmers along his route. Then he turned his wagon back home and poured all the milk into a large can and set it in the stone well in our basement. It was cool there.*
>
> *The next day, Dad set off on his customer route with the entire store of cooled milk resting in the back of the wagon. The customer would come out to meet him with a jug or two in hand and pay him for what she wanted.*

The business filled a need in the community and was a successful one. Then local government got in the way. A health bylaw was passed in Waterloo County that required all milk be pasteurized and bottled under sanitary conditions. "Dad couldn't afford the cost of the pasteurizing equipment, so he sold the business to a relative," Vera recalls. In any case, this ended Henry Good's career as a country milkman.

Disappointed but undaunted, Henry moved on to business number three. On his milk rounds, he had noticed garbage piling up along roadsides and driveways. The unsightly roadside refuse blotted the beauty of the country but gave Henry a bright idea. He would start a garbage pickup business. "Once a week, he'd arrive at area houses and farms, and take away the household waste. People paid for that service, too," states Vera.

Once again bureaucracy put the kibosh on Henry Good's entrepreneurship. Waterloo local officials decreed that garbage pickup would now be a civic responsibility, and they invited bids from citizens who wanted to be considered for the job. "Dad put his bid in, but it was too high and the job was awarded to another bidder," says Vera.

At least two of Henry Good's ventures brought more problems than income. One summer Henry went into raising turkeys. Some of the birds would be ready to butcher for Thanksgiving, with the rest ready by Christmas. The turkeys preferred roosting for the night in the pine trees across from the Good family home. Once the sun rose they strutted across the road for morning feeding. One morning the birds failed to return from their overnight accommodation. A quick walk across the road revealed the reason. "Someone who had noticed where the turkeys spent the night stole every last one of them," explains Vera. The loss of income was devastating to the family – worse with Christmas on the horizon.

Another of Henry's ventures resulted in more than a loss of income. In an effort to bring more money into the family coffers, Henry had rented out part of his barn to an acquaintance. What the renter told Henry he'd be storing in the upper floor of the barn is lost to history. But the arrival of the police at the Good door one day, demanding to see inside the barn, indicated that something shady was going on. Inspection of the loft located a quantity of bootleg liquor hidden under the straw. The police were soon satisfied that Henry had had nothing to do with the crime and set off in search of the bootlegger. But the repercussions were considerable for the Good family. As word of the shenanigans spread throughout the community, it inevitably reached the church. At the next Sunday service Henry was publically shamed. "It was a humiliating experience for us – especially Father," admits Vera. One wonders if Henry had second thoughts about his re-entrance into the church family after this minor brush with the law.

6
On to School

Now a centenarian, Vera steps outside her present self to paint a picture of Vera the pre-schooler. "I was very curious and probably strong-willed, too. When Erma and I played school on the landing of our house, I was always the teacher; Erma was always the pupil. I liked telling her what to do!" Her opinionated nature at times rankled her siblings.

> *I can't remember the cause, but on one occasion I'd annoyed Milton enough for him to give me a slap. Father saw what happened and was horrified. He made Milton apologize, which my brother readily did. But thinking back on it, I'm sure I'd done something awful to annoy him. Milton wasn't a bully.*

As a child, young Vera liked to insert herself into adult conversations, too. "I liked adding my two cents' worth when adults were talking." By the time she was four, she had already begun to think ahead. "Miss Hall-man, the teacher, walked by our house every Friday afternoon on her way home. And just about every time I saw her I asked the same question: 'When will I be old enough to go to school? Can I start school soon?'" "Soon, child," the kindly teacher would answer. Over the coming decades, Vera Good's enthusiasm for learning would never diminish.

Finally in September 1921, Vera followed her older sisters and brother to S.S. #25, Bearinger School, just north of the ever-growing town of Waterloo.[16] Bearinger was a one-room school, without electricity during Vera's years. Coal-oil lamps were lit on dark, dismal days. Eight grades, with around thirty pupils in total – primarily a mixture of Old Order and moderate Mennonite families like the Goods – were taught by one teacher barely out of high school herself. No mean task for a teenager!

Most of the children arrived at school speaking either Pennsylvania Dutch or Low German – the languages spoken in most homes. Given their background, the children would have preferred to speak their first language on the playground, too. But teachers at little one-room schools like S.S. #25 had been given strict directives from their school board to discourage this. The teachers had various ways of catching those disobeying the law.

One teacher, while I was attending Bearinger School, set up a spy system and asked us to report on our friends if we heard violations. When the kids were caught, they had their names marked down on the blackboard. More violations and they got check-marks beside their name. When the checks reached a certain number, the kids had to write out multiple times: "I must not speak Pennsylvania Dutch in school."

One punishment, Vera adds, usually did the trick.

As a school starter, Vera was an astute observer. She took notice of the qualities that were necessary for one teacher to wrangle more than thirty students, from the primary grades through to grade 8 graduation. "Above all, I saw that a teacher needed to be well-organized. She had to figure out how to keep a lot of children busy, all by herself." Vera also picked up a few tricks of the trade of a one-room schoolteacher. "Social studies, music, and health lent themselves to grouping grades together. This was efficient and the younger kids learned from the older ones. But mathematics and reading needed to be taught sequentially."

Even at this age, Vera was able to recognize the amount of work that teaching in a one-room schoolhouse took. Still, she could see herself one day at the front of a classroom. But curiously, not as a teacher of children but as a "teacher of teachers."

So I asked my teacher, Miss Hallman, how I could do this – be a teacher who taught teachers. She was patient with me and told me that I should write a letter to the Minister of Education in Toronto to get an answer. So I did and told him that I had always wanted to be a teacher of teachers, and how should I go about this?

While Vera has no indication that the letter she received back was actually from the Great Man Himself (or if he had even read it), one fine day, a reply with the return address of the Ontario Department of Education offices arrived at the Good home. "I was so excited when Mother gave me the letter to open. It told me I should become a teacher of children first; then I could go on after that to teach teachers." This response was cause enough to give Vera inspiration throughout the rest of her years of elementary school.

Little could Vera, or Miss Hallman for that matter, have predicted that one day Dr. Vera Good would come to know the Minister of Education personally.

7
Ready for the Next Step

In 1929, Vera was ready to graduate from Bearinger School. In these gritty years of the Great Depression, few grade 8 graduates would carry on to high
school. With times tough, most would be counted on to
find work to help support the family.

Even if family finances allowed graduates to carry
on to higher learning, there were two interim steps
they would first need to master. Grade 8 graduates who
wanted to continue their schooling would need to be
nominated by their teachers as worthy; then they would
need to "sit" the daunting province-wide departmental
exam. Only those who passed were allowed to continue
to the hallowed halls of higher learning.

With Vera's long-term goal still firmly rooted, she
eagerly anticipated being allowed to take the test. "I
liked writing tests," she laughs, "I was good at them." Of
Bearinger School's graduating class of 1929, only three
students were recommended by their teacher to write

the entrance exam.

> *One of them was me, and I was so excited. But a day before the exam, something truly horrible happened. My sister Edna came down with the measles. This meant that all of my brothers and sisters still in school, me included, had to be quarantined at home for several days. So I couldn't write the departmental exams. I was absolutely crushed.*

Vera's teacher, in consultation with her school inspector, came up with a creative solution to the problem. "Over all eight grades the three of us had always been ranked #1, #2, and #3 in the class. So what they decided to do was that if both my classmates passed the exam, then I would too!" The news was good coming out of the departmental exam. While only two Bearinger School students had written the exam and had passed it, three were given permission to move on.

However, the drama made no difference to Vera's situation. Her parents' decision was firm. Like her sisters before her, and according to Mennonite custom, Vera would be working at home come September. Stoically accepting tradition, Vera still admits that her last walk home from school was an emotional one. "I wanted to go to high school so badly, so I could follow my dream to be a teacher of teachers. But I also respected our family's tradition."

8
At Home

At home, Vera's duties saw her assisting her mother with housework and caring for her younger siblings, Robert and Harold, who were still pre-schoolers. She missed learning as much as she missed the social interaction of school. As 1929 passed into 1930 and her year at home drew to a close, Vera now anticipated the inevitability of following Viola, Lorene, and Edna into factory work. Viola had been toiling for eight years, Lorene six years, and Edna a year behind treadle sewing machines at the Forsyth Shirt Company in Kitchener.

One of the largest employers in Kitchener, Forsyth, founded in 1903, had begun its business life manufacturing thread, buckles, and sweat pads. In 1914 the company branched out into pyjamas, then men's shirts. By the late 1920s, when the Good girls were employed, the factory was a going concern with over 500 employees.[17]

Still, in her heart of hearts, Vera continued to

hope that her wish to become a teacher might hold sway with her parents, and they might allow her to continue her education. After all, ability had changed the course of her older brother Milton's life. She dared to hope the same for herself.

Milton Good had avoided the stay-at-home-to-farm fate that most Mennonite boys shouldered. "Milton was so smart and was so good at figures that my parents agreed to his going to Kitchener Collegiate Institute and Vocational School (KCI) for the three-year commercial program," says Vera. It was a decision that could bring only financial benefits to the hard-strapped family.

At age seventeen, Milton graduated from his commercial program and was hired to a junior position at the Royal Bank in Kitchener. Over the coming years, Milton Good's paycheque was a godsend to his family. But then, Milton was a boy and a smart boy at that. Vera didn't dare hope her own abilities and expectations would hold sway with tradition-bound parents. What Vera didn't know was that she had a champion – an unlikely one at that – right under her roof!

Viola's Influence

It was Vera's oldest sister, Viola, who offered unexpected support for Vera's ambitions. Vera recalls overhearing her older sibling lobbying their parents on her behalf.

> *Viola started to try to pressure Mom and Dad to let me go to high school like Milton had. It was a surprise because Viola, who was eight years older than me, wasn't the sibling I was closest to. We got along but weren't best friends like Erma and Edna were with me. No doubt my own life story would have been far different if it hadn't been for Viola.*

What Vera didn't know at the time was that her oldest sister was chafing at her own fate. "I found out later that she didn't want the same life for me as the one she had been living for years and years."

Born in 1907, Viola Good was a serious child with a strong devotion to family and faith.[18] Like Vera, in her youth Viola had longed to be a teacher. But in the early years of the century in devout Mennonite families like the Goods, the place for women was in the home, or in fulfilling menial tasks such as housekeeping or factory work.

And so after her at-home year, Viola was hired out for a year to several Mennonite families as a mother's helper and cleaner. In 1923, at age sixteen, she joined the sewers at the Forsyth Shirt Company in Kitchener. Lorene and Edna followed. For the Good girls, work began before they stepped a foot onto the factory floor. "The walk from home to Forsyth in downtown Kitchener was at least five miles each way. My sisters would do it rain, winds, and snow. Only if there was a howling blizzard would Dad hitch the horses to the cutter and drive them." And, Vera adds, "they didn't complain. It was just the way it was and what people of that generation expected." Following Mennonite tradition, the girls' income passed into the family coffers, and it would continue to do so until they reached the age of twenty-one. At that point independence could be gained.

Viola, still living at home at age twenty-two, was now building herself a little nest egg and making efforts to fulfill her own dreams. Once the road was cleared for

Vera to return to school, she planned to leave Forsyth for Toronto and the Toronto Bible School.

As the oldest, Viola's words carried some weight with Henry and Mary Good, and after considerable discussion they decided that Vera would follow Milton to high school. In doing so, she would be the first girl of her family to reach past grade 8. What wasn't decided was which program Vera would enter. "Viola felt that I should go into the academic program at high school – thinking that I had the abilities to maybe even go on to college or university." As much as Vera still harboured goals of being "a teacher of teachers," this road seemed impractical given the economic times.

> *The Great Depression was hitting families hard and mine was no exception. It was my older sisters' and brother's financial contributions from their jobs that kept our family afloat. And I wanted to be a part of that too. So if I was going to go to high school, it had to be in the three-year commercial program like Milton had taken, not the five-year academic one. With this I could get a decent job in an office.*

And teaching? That was only a fond pipe dream in a hazy future.

In September 1930, Vera registered in KCI's commercial program. "So I disappointed my oldest sister," Vera admits, "and not for the last time."

10

Kitchener Collegiate

With school busses still a distant dream for the Kitchener School Board, Vera and two S.S. #25 friends, Hilda and Rita Bearinger, walked the four-mile distance from their homes on the northern reaches of the town of Waterloo to Kitchener Collegiate on King Street in Kitchener. "It took us just less than an hour each way, but we didn't complain," offers Vera, matter-of-factly. "We just did it." She didn't complain about her lack of a school social life, either. "Many of my classmates took part in the extracurricular life of high school – singing in the choir, playing sports, or other activities. For me, high school meant classes. Period. School was just a means to an end, and the sooner the better."

Before long, the means to Vera's end had become an exercise in frustration. "The content of the classes was quite easy for me. And it didn't take too long before I was feeling bored." The thought of a full three years of typing, shorthand, and business practice weighed heavily on her. And she needed to do something about it.

> So I made an appointment to talk to the school
> principal, Mr. R.N. Merritt.[19] I hoped that he could
> find a solution to my situation. After I was shown
> into Mr. Merritt's office, I said to him: "I really don't
> want to spend three years in school when I could be
> learning the work in a much shorter time. I want
> to get out in the workforce as soon as I can, so I can
> help my family."

Impressed with the teenager's argument, not to mention her initiative, Principal Merritt permitted Vera to switch into the one-year commercial program midstream when she returned for a second year. If she kept up with the pace, she would graduate at the end of two years instead of three. "He did warn me that I'd get less material in the one-year course of study. But that was fine with me."

In June of 1932, Vera Good left Kitchener Collegiate with a commercial certificate. With her businesslike attitude and strong academic abilities, it didn't take her long to find a job. She was hired by Kaufman Rubber in Kitchener to work in their office. Invoicing was Vera's primary work duty.

In a nod to Viola, Vera also began work on academic home study which would, if she stuck with it, give her a grade 12 graduation certificate. The kindly Mr. Merritt had provided her with textbooks and facilitated several teachers to act as resources for her. After settling into her job at Kaufman, Vera spent her evenings studying mathematics, history, and English literature. "Teaching was still a goal," she says. "But at this point, it seemed as unlikely as taking a trip to the moon."

11
First Crush

At Kaufman Rubber, Vera was content in her office job. "It was a pleasant place to work, with a fair boss (A.R. Kaufman), and there were nice people in my department." Still, the general office work that filled her days was well below her capabilities. No matter. Especially in those bleak years of the Great Depression, work was work.

At the same time, Vera kept the teaching dream in the back of her mind as she settled down each evening to several hours of home study. Sailing easily through grade 9, 10, 11, and 12 modules of English, history, and geography, Vera had more difficulty with mathematics. "I could do the other subjects completely independently," Vera recalls, "but math was more difficult. I was a bit concerned whether I'd get through it."

Eventually, Vera discovered a source of assistance (and more) at a Bearinger School Christmas concert. One year, while attending the seasonal festivities at her old school with her sisters, she met the current teacher, Mr. Jim Colton. In conversation with him during the social part of the evening, Vera mentioned her home studies – in particular her mathematics challenges. "He told me he was good in math and would gladly come to my house to tutor me. No payment expected. Maybe a snack would be welcome, though!" Vera eagerly accepted.

The two got along well and before long, Vera had developed a crush on her young tutor. "After we'd finished working, I'd go into the kitchen and make some food for us. Jim's favourite was grilled cheese and bacon under the broiler." Occasionally, when the weather was fine, they would go for a walk or take in a movie before Jim returned home. Vera still thinks of Jim as "my first love. I was very fond of him." For two years they worked on her mathematics as, lesson by lesson, Vera made her way through the grades.

Near the end of Vera's grade 12 home study year, Jim Colton brought painful news. He was resigning his position at S.S. #25 and would be heading to the University of Western Ontario to begin his university degree.[20] Vera was devastated. "I never quite got over Jim; and I certainly never forgot him." This relationship letdown was compounded by a work disappointment. Vera had now been at Kaufman Rubber for ten years, and when an upper-level secretarial position opened up – one for which she felt well qualified – she planned to apply. She decided to tell her supervisor first, not realizing this would lead to some behind-the-scenes dealing that followed her announcement:

> *My supervisor ... wanted me to stay in my position in invoicing. So he used some pressure on the head boss to make sure I didn't get the job. And I didn't. This really crushed my spirit, since I was clearly the best candidate for the position. In the end, though, it turned out for the best.*

It was a serendipitous turning point in Vera Good's life. She had completed all the courses needed to earn her grade 12 graduation diploma and decided that now was the time to fulfill the dream she had carried with her since childhood.

12
A Full-Time High School Student

Only one barrier stood in Vera's way to becoming a teacher. To be admitted to Normal School (teacher's college), she would need to complete senior matriculation, or grade 13. Since home study wasn't an option for this step up the education ladder, Vera would now need to attend school full-time. "That was no financial problem for me. I'd worked for ten years and had saved some money. And as far as fitting in with my classmates, this didn't bother me one bit."

In August 1942, Vera gave her notice at Kaufman Rubber, and in September, she walked through the doors of Kitchener Collegiate as a full-time high school student. No doubt the kindly Principal Merritt, still at the helm of Kitchener's only public high school, was delighted to see her. At age twenty-seven, now older than most of her peers by a decade, she rolled up her sleeves and got down to work. The results surely reinforced what older sister Viola had seen in her younger sister:

Vera's grades were exceptional.

In June 1943, Vera Good graduated from Kitchener Collegiate as the top student of her class. There
had been a few side trips along the way, but Vera was
now poised to move on to the next chapter of her life
– Stratford Normal School. Or was she? A letter she
received near the end of the school year put her in some
doubt about her destination.

13

Here? Or Here?

Fulfilling a lifelong goal was on the horizon for Vera. She had been accepted to Stratford Normal School, and to make the offer even sweeter, she had been awarded a $100 entrance scholarship. It was an honour past her wildest dreams. Then a letter arrived bearing the postmark of Elkhart, Indiana. Vera recalls her curiosity as she opened the mystery missive. "The letter was offering me admission to Goshen College. It shocked me because I hadn't even applied there. I was sure somehow Viola had been behind the offer."

Here we'll pause briefly in Vera's story to again turn our sights on Viola Good. When we left her in 1930, Viola was toiling as a seamstress at the Forsyth

Shirt Company in Kitchener. At home she was urging her parents to allow Vera the opportunity to follow a different path than her own. With Vera's successful return to education, Viola felt compelled to do the same. In a personal essay called "My Pilgrimage," Viola wrote: "I made such a decision to go back to school at age 22, after six years on a factory treadmill. I feel I could not have done that, given the obstacles in my way, except for the special impulse of a power outside of myself."[21]

After Viola resigned from Forsyth, she enrolled in the three-year program at Toronto Bible School, boarding with a Christian family near campus. For a reserved, small-town girl, the move to Toronto must initially have been a traumatic one. Following her graduation, Viola returned home and took up her former job at Forsyth. But this would be a briefer stay. Viola had purpose in her return to factory work, for she had also applied to Goshen Mennonite College and would first need to save up some money. Viola, a long-range planner like Vera, had previously taken several Goshen extension courses in the hopes that one day she would be admitted to the respected Mennonite college as a full-time student.

In 1936, a light shone at the end of Viola Good's long tunnel. Goshen President S.C. Yoder had become aware of Viola's aspirations through her correspondence courses and through her application to work with the Mennonite Mission Board. Yoder was impressed by the young woman's perseverance and invited her to come to Goshen College to continue her full-time education there. Aware that tuition and board costs would likely preclude Viola's accepting his invitation, Yoder offered her the position of Matron of Kulp Hall, the girls' residence at Goshen. She would live in the dormitory to fulfill her matron's duties, while also attending classes. Viola left Waterloo for Goshen in 1936.

It was surely through Viola that the invitation to Goshen had come. "And once again I disappointed my sister," Vera says with a sigh. "I felt I had to turn it down."

> *Being admitted to a respected college like Goshen was an honour, to be sure, and I was tempted. The chance to be near Viola appealed to me, too. But being offered a scholarship to Normal School was a distinction. Also, Normal School was a more direct way to reach my teaching goal. If I'd gone to Goshen for a BA, I still would have had to go to Normal School after that.*

At the mature age of twenty-eight, Vera was in a rush. After much soul-searching, she turned the Goshen invitation down.

14
Stratford Normal School

Surely the source of considerable hilarity among non-academics – "Teachers have to go to a school to become normal?" – the word "normal" had nothing to do with a would-be teacher's state of being. The term is derived from the French *école normale*, and refers to model schools and classrooms that had been integral to French educational training for generations.[22]

Even by the time Vera Good attended Stratford Normal School in the mid-1940s, teacher training in Ontario lagged far behind that in the United States and Western Europe. Without the leadership of one Egerton Ryerson a century before Vera achieved her teacher training, the gap would surely have been considerably greater.[23]

The training of Ontario teachers had been the "brainchild" of Methodist minister and politician Egerton Ryerson. Ryerson was a forward thinker who called education "as necessary as the light – it should be as common as water and as free as air."

Charged by Lt. Governor of Upper Canada Charles Metcalf in 1844, Ryerson left Canada on a fact-finding mission to observe education systems and teacher training institutions around the world. He returned full of ideas for immediate action.

In 1846, Ryerson's Common Schools Act was passed in the Legislature of Upper Canada. The most significant of Ryerson's recommendations was the founding of Normal Schools. At the time, no certification or training was required to teach elementary school in what would become the province of Ontario. In most cases, grammar school (high school) teachers had attended university but had no pedagogical training. A library in every school and textbooks written by Canadian authors were also on Egerton Ryerson's "must-have" list.

It took only one year after Ryerson's report for Upper Canada's first teacher-training institution to open. The Toronto Normal School at St. James Square was founded in 1847. To be admitted, applicants needed to have attained their sixteenth birthday, provide a certificate of good moral character from a clergyman, and demonstrate clear evidence of reading, writing, and arithmetic achievement. Twenty young men began five months of instruction in St. James's first year of operation. They were succeeded in 1848 by a class of 118, including twenty women

Four additional Normal Schools followed: in North Bay, Hamilton, Peterborough, and Stratford. Curiously, each building, designed in the Italian Renaissance style, was identical in size, shape, and building materials to the others.

More measures followed over the succeeding decades. With the School Act of 1871, all Ontario children were granted the right to an elementary education. With this, the student population of Ontario schools increased dramatically. As a response, the Ottawa Normal School opened in 1875, followed by the London Normal School in 1900. As the century turned, 8,321 teachers had been educated to teach in Ontario schools.

The loss of male teachers to the war effort from 1939 to 1945 brought thousands of women into the teaching ranks. Such was the demand for teachers that during the war, summer sessions were added to accommodate student teachers.

This was the status quo when Vera Good was admitted to the Stratford Normal School in 1943.[24]

On her arrival in Stratford, Vera's first task was to find a boarding house. She settled on the Stratford

Young Women's Christian Association (YWCA). The "Y" was Canada's oldest institution to provide accommodation for women, and popular with young working women and students.[25] Built in 1928 on Waterloo Street in midtown, the two-storey "Y" was modest in price and "respectable." Boarders could rent single or double rooms, or opt for the least expensive rate with dormitory accommodation. In a dormitory room, each boarder was provided with a single bed, a small bedside table, and a lamp for late-night reading or studying.

A dormitory room would suit the unpretentious Vera just fine. But not if the YWCA matron had anything to do with it! One look at Miss Good, in her late twenties, convinced the caretaker that this mature boarder would not be happy in a lively, noisy dorm with "kids." Vera recalls: "The matron decided that I'd be better rooming with an older woman who had a double room to herself. So she put me there. And I didn't like the arrangement at all."

The isolation from the other girls, many of whom were her classmates at Normal School, was bad enough, but then Vera discovered that she and her roommate had nothing in common. The "strange, dark pictures" on the woman's wall were the clincher.

So I asked to be moved to the dorm with the kids. And yes, it was certainly noisier than the double room, but it didn't bother me in the least. My bed was in a corner off to the side and I worked long

*after the other girls had gone to sleep. I thoroughly
enjoyed the fellowship of the other women and it
was a wonderful year.*

On weekends Vera went home to Waterloo. With
two other Normal School students, she rode with Stratford Master Gerhardt Dobrint. Dobrint was on a leave
from his regular job as Inspector of Schools with the
Department of Education in Waterloo, and was happy
to have some company along for the ride to and from
Stratford. Little could Vera have known how valuable
Mr. G.E. Dobrint would become when it came time to
search for a teaching job.

15
Riverbank School

As the term drew to a close at Stratford Normal School, Vera remained optimistic about finding a teaching job. "I think my confidence stemmed from the fact that I was a mature new teacher and my maturity showed." She had done "very well" in her practice teaching opportunities. Vera's optimism turned to celebration when her congenial driver, Gerhardt Dobrint, offered her a teaching job.

> *As an experienced school inspector, Mr. Dobrint had gained a very good idea of what made a successful teacher. And I guess he had seen that in me over the close to a year I rode with him from Stratford to Waterloo. He thought I'd be well suited to teach at Riverbank Public School outside Breslau, just east of Kitchener. It had a student population of around thirty pupils, from grades 1 to 8, and I'd teach them all!*

Miss Good would be acting as school principal, too. She laughs in recalling her assignment: "I wouldn't call it a plum job, but it *was* a job and it was mine – without even having to go to an interview!" Her pay would amount to $1200 a school year. "I took the job without even seeing the inside of it. It didn't really matter to me, really. I was just thrilled to have the job."

Vera didn't get a first look at her school until mid-August, when she had arranged to do some organizing work in the classroom. With no transportation to get herself to Riverbank, a good ten miles from her home in the north end of Waterloo, she took a bus out to Breslau, east of the growing city of Kitchener. But she needed to make one quick stop before she continued down the road to the school. "I walked to the Breslau general store, where I presented myself as the new teacher. I'd been told I could pick up a key to open the door to the school there. Then I walked the rest of the way to Riverbank."

Vera liked what she saw. Built in 1832, S.S. #15 Riverbank School, formerly High Banks School, was one of the oldest in Waterloo County.[26] Originally constructed of logs, then modernized with wood frame, by Vera's time the school was enduring the elements with a solid face of granite. Only the occasional overflowing of the nearby Grand River prompted yearly reminders of caution from Riverbank's school teachers.

Vera's excitement bubbled as she turned the key to enter "her" school. "There was so much I wanted to accomplish before I caught the bus back home that I hardly knew where to start. So I started by taking an inventory of what I had on hand in the supply cupboard, and what I needed to order. The day flew by and I needed to leave." Decorating the building entrance and her classroom would have to wait until she returned again the day before school opened.

Vera had one more task to accomplish before she walked back to the bus stop. Down the road from the school was the farm of Lloyd and Bertha Hagey and their two young children. The Hagey farm would be her boarding house over the coming school year. Vera recalls her thoughts as she approached the Hagey farmhouse. "'What if I didn't like it here? What if the children were too noisy? What if my room didn't suit?' My heart was thudding as I knocked on the door. Within a few minutes I knew I'd been worrying for nothing. I knew I'd be happy there."

Reflecting on her two years as the Hagey family's boarder, Vera's fondest memories involve conversations at the dining room table. "Lloyd Hagey was an intelligent and knowledgeable man who kept the conversation lively around the dinner table. He raised hogs and dairy cattle and was quite involved with the Farmers'

Club. It was a social organization that gave farmers a chance to mix with their neighbours." When there were social functions at the Farmers' Club, Lloyd Hagey encouraged Vera to attend with the family. "It gave me a chance to meet the community and talk to adults instead of just children. It was great."

Breakfasts offered Vera other amusements. Lloyd and his hired man ate early and left for the barn before Vera was up and getting ready for school. This left baby Becky, in her high chair, as Vera's usual table companion. "Becky was just starting to talk and would say the funniest things. If she saw me slouching at the table she'd scold me, telling me to 'get up, Vi-Vi.'"

16
A Day on the Job

Vera was an accomplished organizer and from the beginning, she managed her classroom expertly. "My years in the office at Kaufman Rubber stood me in good stead, thank goodness. I'd need to be organized to survive thirty-two students in eight different grades." She recalls her charges as "mostly farm kids, respectful and well-behaved." Vera knew full well that she was fortunate not to have any students with hard-core behaviour problems.

I think I gave one student the strap over my two years there. I regretted strapping that boy the minute I did it, and I probably only managed three slaps. Afterward I told myself that this was not the type of teacher I wanted to be, and that I'd never strap another student. In the end the strapping hurt me much more than it did the young boy.

A bigger challenge for Vera, as it was for all one-room schoolteachers, was covering the curriculum for all eight grades as set down by Ontario's Department of Education. While some subjects like social studies, geography, and health lent themselves to grouping (as she had observed during her student days in a one-room school), the core subjects of arithmetic and reading needed to be targeted to the correct age group and grade. Vera was aware that some teachers felt they needed help to cover all bases.

> *Some teachers in one-room schools depended on senior students. But I had no interest in using them to teach the little ones and only did it occasionally. My feeling was that teachers who did this were taking advantage of the older ones — depriving them of their own learning experiences. To me it was like taking them hostage.*

In Vera Good's classroom, senior students played a much more important role than being unpaid teaching assistants. "The seniors modelled behaviour for the little ones – what was appropriate, what wasn't." Vera had noticed that primary-grade youngsters in such a mixed environment interacted better with all age groups. And they seemed to be more mature than children she had seen in multi-room schools.

Still, keeping track of eight grades herself had its disadvantages. "I'd excuse myself right after supper at the Hageys, and head up to my room to start planning lessons for the next day. And I'd usually work well into the night." Still, she missed the dining-room table banter led by Lloyd Hagey and occasionally let planning wait.

One lesson for which Miss Good didn't have to prepare was music. Each week an itinerant music teacher assigned to cover all the one-room schools across the county arrived. This travelling teacher would introduce the students to a new song or two, then leave instructions for the class to practice till she returned the next week.

Physical education was low maintenance, too. With no formal curriculum or gymnasium at Riverbank, Miss Good routinely led her class in doing stretches and bends beside their desks. Warm weather made it easier, as the children moved outside for team sports like softball. "And I insisted that the boys let the girls play with them too."

Outdoor recess gave teachers like Vera a welcome break from wrangling active youngsters. Incidents on the school playground were few, and students could generally be trusted to being on their own in the school yard. The sight of teachers on yard duty, patrolling the school playground, was many years in the future. The status quo changed during miserable weather, when students were relegated to the school basement for recess. "Now that was an ordeal," Vera admits.

Since her own school days, Vera had been a great

fan of the Christmas concert. Now she eagerly looked forward to planning this annual rite herself. "Back then, for very little money, you could buy a play from a publishing company that included enough parts for a class the size of mine." And for the musically inclined? The inevitable Christmas carols put everyone in the holiday spirit. Not only did parents and relatives of Riverbank students show up in droves for the Christmas performance, but also members of neighbouring communities. "Everybody wanted to see what everybody else was doing and rate it with what they were doing in their own school."

Vera returned to Riverbank for a second year. And while she would rank the encore as even better than her first year of teaching, over the year she began to have a change of heart.

> *I very much liked teaching and I'd had a good experience to start. So I wasn't dissatisfied – not in the least. But I was now close to thirty years of age. And I really had never been away from home and family. I felt that I needed a change; I needed to add a new dimension to my life. And, at my age, I'd better do it sooner than later if it was going to happen at all.*

With regret, Vera handed in her resignation in the spring of 1946. Her major concern on leaving Riverbank was what the response in the community would be. "I was sure people would say: 'She waited all those years to become a teacher and she's gone after only two years? What's the matter with that girl?'"

But, says Vera, "I had every intention of returning to the classroom after a couple of years of doing something else." She had a pretty good idea of what that "something else" would be – and it would involve some travel.

PART TWO

Foreign Service

(1946–1949)

17
Vera's Assignment

It turns out that Vera's decision to leave River-bank, a school she loved, after two years was not that unusual among the one-room teacher set. "Many teachers who had similar assignments to mine requested a new placement after two years – some earlier. It was a heavy load we carried and most of us needed to move on."

"Moving on" for Vera was taking a foreign service placement with the Mennonite Central Committee (MCC). In this respect, she joined many of her faith. Still, at age thirty-one, she was a bit older than most MCC workers, who had done their service after high school or university. But Vera Good was no less enthusiastic a recruit than her younger counterparts. MCC offered adventure, valuable practical experience, and above all, it fulfilled a Mennonite's pledge of service to others.[27]

Founded in 1920 in Chicago, Illinois, the Mennonite Central Committee was originally formed as a response to pleas from Mennonites living in the southern part of Russia (now Ukraine). Thousands of men, women, and children had been reduced to starvation through drought and persecution by Josef Stalin's Red Army. Over the worst years of the persecution, from 1922 to 1923, MCC relief workers provided an estimated 75,000 meals each day to their Russian sisters and brothers.

MCC was galvanized into action again in Poland during World War II. The country had been overrun by two invading armies – Germany moving east, Russia moving west. Millions of Mennonites fleeing westward were fed during these dark days. MCC also had "non-partisan" relief workers stationed in England, Germany, and France.

After the end of the war in 1945, MCC turned its attention to rising conflicts elsewhere in the world. Relief workers were sent to post-war Egypt, China, and India. India had the potential to be the area of the most savage of conflicts. As the British-held colony moved toward independence, violence between Hindus, Muslims, and Sikhs escalated.

In the late 1950s, MCC began to build a strong Voluntary Service program. Its target was young Americans as well as Canadians, encouraging them to perform service in underdeveloped countries of the world. Over the coming decades, MCC volunteers worked to improve education, housing, health, farming/agriculture methods, and infrastructure for resources such as water in developing nations.

In 1963, a Canadian arm of MCC was organized out of the binational MCC office in Akron, Pennsylvania. Before that time, Vera and other young Canadian Mennonites wishing to volunteer for overseas service had to do so through MCC in the United States.[28]

Vera hoped that her professional expertise could be put to good use during her two-year term with MCC. "I thought that given my teacher's training, I'd be best posted to a European country where students were learning English, like in France or Germany or Spain." When she received her marching orders – three years' service instead of two, and to India instead of Western Europe – she was surprised. And a little disappointed! "The first thought I had was how my teacher training was going to assist me in a country like India, where English wasn't routinely taught. My second thought was that three years is a long, long time to be away!"

Vera smiles, remembering the response she received from MCC when she questioned the terms of her placement. "They advised me to 'trust in the Lord.' So if I wanted to do volunteer service, I really didn't have a lot of options beyond that!"

18

"Trusting in the Lord"

At the same time that Vera was preparing to leave Canada, the Good family was anxiously waiting the return of son and brother Robert from the battlefields of Europe. As a Mennonite pacifist, Robert Good could have chosen to serve his country through Alternative Service instead of combat. Most Mennonite men of conscription age participated in Alternative Service during the war years, serving on farms, assisting with food production, working in lumber camps or in factories. "But Robert's choice had been to fight," says Vera. She was greatly relieved to receive word after she departed for India that her younger brother had indeed arrived home.

In late August 1946, Vera left Kitchener by train
for Akron, Pennsylvania, the headquarters of the Mennonite Central Committee. Travelling with her was
Elaine Snyder, a young nurse from Waterloo. She was
also heading into service in India. In Akron, the two
Canadians would take orientation sessions to prepare
themselves for their upcoming mission.

Elaine had been informed that she would be
working directly with refugees in the Indian relief
camps. The number of displaced people had multiplied
as independence neared and sectarian violence escalated.
Vera, on the other hand, remained in the dark about
what she would be doing over her term of service. "It
was a bit unnerving not knowing, seeing as most people
I'd met knew their [assignment]."

On September 26, 1946, Vera and Elaine boarded
a ship bound for Naples, Italy. The vessel had done service transporting American troops across the Atlantic to
the war in Europe. In the Canadians' party were ap-
proximately twenty-five missionaries and relief workers,
including eight children. Calm waters made the Atlantic crossing uneventful. On schedule, the ship briefly
docked in Naples. Those headed to India now boarded a
smaller ship, which would cross the Mediterranean Sea
and disembark at Alexandria, Egypt.

From Alexandria, they boarded a train bound for

Cairo, remaining there for several days until transportation to the Indian subcontinent was arranged. Vera has clear memories of the train journey between Alexandria and Cairo, a distance of about 120 miles. "It was like you see in a movie – private compartments for the first-class passengers, each with usually four people to a compartment, with train staff to assist you with any need you had."

For the first-class travellers – which included Vera and Elaine – civility also reached to the train's cooling system. Windows opened to the outside and fans were installed to help with ventilation, too. "And ventilation we sure needed," states Vera. "Egypt was hotter than our hottest weather in Canada." Not so comfortable were the second- and third-class passengers, crammed onto benches in non-ventilated cars.

19

Cairo – and More Cairo

Plans called for Vera and Elaine to remain in Cairo for a week before carrying on to Karachi on the shore of the Indian subcontinent. There were no complaints from either of them for this delay. "We'd been put up in this very luxurious hotel, with tile floors and big chandeliers, and there were servants to look after all our needs," Vera remembers. They could also take advantage of the delay to do some sightseeing in historic Cairo. A trip to the Pyramids and the Sphinx was a must-see. They also took a camel ride: "Sixty cents for an hour," says Vera.

Visits to the open-air markets were eye-opening for the two "country girls." "You could buy pretty well anything you wanted – live chickens, fruit, vegetables, clothing, jewellery, and every kind of bric-a-brac under the sun." Vera thought Cairo market prices "expensive." "Twenty cents for candy that would be a nickel at home." She remembers the fresh dates and Egyptian ice cream as particularly divine. Watching a line of money-changers trying to outdo each other for customers was also good for at least thirty minutes of fun.

By the end of the week, the women were anxious to be on their way. But a week stretched to two, then three, as they anxiously wait for the call. The delay was expensive for MCC, which was putting up its new volunteers in a swanky Cairo hotel and covering their meals. Heading into the fourth week of delay, Vera and Elaine finally received word that they would be covering the last leg of their trip by sea plane. Vera has vivid memories of their "escape" from the mayhem of the Egyptian capital. "Elaine and I left in the dead of night. Our guide was a towering, white-frocked Arab wearing a wide red sash and a fez. He seemed out of a movie, too."

A nasty surprise waited them when they reached the airport: two small planes instead of one were at the ready. "We were told that there wouldn't be enough room for both of us in one plane. We'd have to fly separately." Upset by this latest snag in their travel plans, the two friends needed to collect themselves and decide what to do. "We'd promised each other that we'd stick together, no matter what. But it was either this or wait in Cairo for who knows how long," says Vera.

Once more "trusting in the Lord," Vera crawled into a small two-seater plane, and Elaine boarded a two-seater boat plane. And they were off: "I closed my eyes as the pilot roared along the runway. Shaking and rumbling, we were in the air."

Next stop: the port of Karachi on the west coast of the British Raj of India.

With no idea if her young companion had landed safely or had crashed into the sea, Vera was driven to a Karachi hotel. There she would spend the night before moving on to the Indian capital of New Delhi. Then finally, on to her destination of Calcutta, in the state of Bengal, eastern India.

Given the bumps in the road since she had left Alexandria, Vera shouldn't have been surprised to encounter another adventure in Karachi. "The hotel was very Eastern – a suite of rooms, opening onto a balcony beneath the stars. But I was too exhausted to appreciate it and I climbed into my bed." Then a movement drew Vera's eyes to the ceiling.

A ring of little chameleons were resting on the ceiling all around the light. I'd never seen chameleons before, and I had no idea if they were dangerous or not. I do admit to being terrified. What if a whole bunch of them jumped down on me in my bed? What if one of them bit me? I'll admit that I got very little sleep that night, but I didn't have any close encounters with the little lizards.

20

Calcutta – Finally

Vera had been assured that someone from MCC would be on hand to meet her when she arrived at Calcutta's Dum-Dum airport. She was disappointed. But always resourceful, Vera looked for a solution to her latest transportation snag. "I found an airport steward who spoke a bit of English, and with my few words of Hindi, we understood each other." With Vera hovering close by, the steward flagged down an open-air taxi with a Sikh driver, and she climbed aboard. And they were off.

"Within a few hundred metres, the driver stopped to give some friends a ride. So now there were three Sikhs crammed in the front and me in the back. It must have looked pretty funny." Once again Vera recalled the "trust in the Lord" conversation in Akron.

Safely, if not soundly, Vera arrived at the MCC offices in Calcutta (known today as Kolkata), a teeming city of close to two million people. The headquarters were located in a United Church Girls' School near the busy Wellington Square in the central district of the city. The building would also serve as living accommodations for the MCC staff. For meals and social meeting times, they'd need to cross the square to the Lee Memorial Mission Building.

Since parting in Cairo, Vera's thoughts had remained on Elaine. "I hoped that all was well. I was worried – a young girl on her own like that." Vera didn't have too long to worry. Elaine appeared within hours of her own arrival. By the next day, she had headed to where she would be working at Dhamtari Hospital.

Vera bided her time for a day or two until her unit leader Martin Schrag, an American, arrived.

> *And so, I finally got my "marching orders" from Martin and knew I'd do just fine. As Martin would be out of the office frequently, I'd be in charge of keeping things running. That would be the usual secretarial jobs: typing, filing, answering telephones. But I'd also be the liaison between MCC and the government, arranging permits and other official communication.*

Gradually, Vera settled into life in the populous Indian city. She admits that some aspects were harder to get used to than others. "The smell coming from the open sewers in Calcutta was pretty hard to take." On the plus side, there was trying out Indian cuisine. Vera readily took to Indian curries and other exotic dishes.

21
India in Turmoil:
Moving to Independence

Vera's posting to India coincided with the climax of the "Free India" movement, which had slowly been gaining steam since Mohandas Ghandi's return to his native land in 1915.[29] After almost 200 years of British rule, from 1757 by the British East India Company, then commencing in 1857 by the British government (Queen Victoria was declared Empress of India in 1857), India was moving to independence.

Most India watchers predicted the transition would not be a smooth one. They feared unprecedented violence as Sikhs, Muslims, and Hindus jostled for power in the new political and social order.[30] One of the most contentious issues was the plan to partition India and its northern province of Pakistan into two self-governing countries. Political planning would see Muslims dominant in Pakistan, with Hindus, Sikhs, and other minority faiths primarily in India.[31]

In a letter of October 21, 1947, to MCC, Vera described a country at war with itself: "There are relief needs in other parts of India but all is somewhat overshadowed by the major upheaval in the Punjab. Amritsar is in the heart of the disturbance and … communication is difficult."[32] And so, humanitarian agencies like the American and French Red Cross and the Mennonite Central Committee were at the ready when the chaos erupted. Most of the MCC contingent who had accompanied Vera to India would be working in refugee camps in the vulnerable parts of the nation.

Vera reflects on the India that she found in 1946. "Indians were a proud and capable people who'd learned very well under the British. On the outside they were deferential to them. On the inside they hated them. They wanted to be in charge of their own country. And who could have blamed them?"

And still the British held on – visibly reluctant to let go of the prize jewel in their crown. They had method in their madness. Outsiders, like Canadian Vera Good, could understand the British arguments against independence and their delay in granting it. "They explained the delay by predicting India would be in chaos if they weren't there to keep law and order. It would be Muslims fighting Hindus, Hindus at the throats of Sikhs, and so on."[33]

22
Moving Bases

After months of delays, India gained its independence from Great Britain on August 15, 1947. MCC staff was ready to assist where help was most needed – in the northern Punjab region, close to the new nation of Pakistan. Packing clothes and provisions, the MCC contingent piled into trucks and set out on the four-day journey from Calcutta to New Delhi. Vera recalls the roads and driving conditions as "almost unpassable" and "dangerous."

Occasionally they were able to find a bed for the night in one of the *dak* bungalows that the British had built as post offices during their stay.[34] If not, they bedded down in sleeping bags in the open, beside the truck. A report filed by Vera to MCC headquarters gives details of their relocation:

> *By noon on November 26, we were ready to leave Calcutta with the weapons carrier and trailer load–*

*ed to capacity. The next five and one half days we
were on the road. It was actually a rare privilege to
drive through almost 1000 miles of India's country-
side. Our heavy load necessitated slow driving but
the roads, on the whole were good and we only had
two flats. One flat necessitated our spending a night
in the open, but since it is India one always carries
one's bedding with one. It wasn't too bad, in fact we
rather enjoyed the novelty.[35]*

Not that MCC and other humanitarian agen-
cies would be the targets of aggression. Still, they were
fully aware that their lives could be in danger indirectly.
"With guns going off all around us, we knew that a
stray bullet might be the end of us."

Other areas along the way caused more concern
for the relief workers. Vera told Akron:

*We organized a small relief project in a village
about fifteen miles out of the city. It was an area
which had been devastated by floods, and the farm
labourers were left with no means of a livehood
[sic]. We secured sufficient rice, some atta, and spices
and oil, took them out to the village and set up a
distribution centre.[36]*

On their arrival in New Delhi, the MCC staff,
one that Vera calls "small" compared to other relief
agencies like the Red Cross, moved into the New Delhi

Constitution House. The sight of the grand building gave Vera pause to ponder.

> *The British stay in India hadn't been solely a take-take situation. They left behind them so much that would assist the new nation, such as a solid infrastructure like roads and modern electricity; also a working telephone system, good schools and competent systems of government, not to mention beautiful buildings like Constitution House.*

The relocation to New Delhi also gave Vera her chance to move out of the office and to the centre of action – the relief camps.

As predicted, outside the Indian capital the situation was dire. Thousands of men, women, and children were crowded into refugee camps. Vera described the scene in a letter to MCC headquarters in Akron. "Fern [an MCC worker] tells of how one morning the camp-site was vacant and by noon 15,000 Muslims with 200 carts – a 19 mile long caravan – moved in."[37]

All refugees needed food, water, and milk for infants. Clothing, towels, and soap came well down the list of urgent needs. Vera remembers her reaction after her first visit to a refugee camp.

> *It was terrible. These refugees were living in completely inadequate conditions – not enough food, not enough tents for them to stay. And the sanitary con-*

*ditions were terrible because there weren't enough
latrines. And of course disease was rampant.*

*Whenever one of the relief trucks carrying
food supplies pulled into the camp, the reaction from
the refugees was "bedlam." It was the most aggressive ones who came out on top during the food and
clothing distribution. The ones who politely waited
got little – or nothing.*

MCC's staff supervised the distribution of rice,
the refugees' staple diet. "We called them rice canteens.
The children would be sent with an empty cup to be
filled and then they'd take it back to be cooked. And
that's all a family had." When nights turned cold, problems of a different sort descended on the refugees. Vera
explained how "in Kashmir the poor people had begun
to collect newspapers to line their beds and stuff down
the inside of their thin cotton rags to protect themselves
against this winter's cold."[38]

When relief workers weren't on the front lines
feeding hungry people, they were clothing the inad-
equately dressed Indians. "Good warm clothing will
bring comfort to some of these unfortunate ones. The
girls are remaking some of the western clothing into
forms more acceptable in the east."[39]

Daily life in an Indian refugee camp gave Vera
pause as she recalled an earlier visit she'd made to the
home of wealthy Indian.

There was such a huge gap between the Indian poor and the Indian rich. I had visited the home of an Indian Member of Parliament some months before. His living room was divided into two cultures: one side featured English furniture and decorating; the other side was Indian – rugs and draperies and reclining sofas. I wondered if the great human disparity would close now that India had gained controlled its own destiny.

Amidst the human suffering, racial hatred, and death, India still remained a spectacularly beautiful country. Occasionally the relief workers were able to step aside from their humanitarian work to breathe the pure air of India outside its teeming cities. In a July 1948 letter to MCC headquarters, Vera described one such diversion.

The valleys and lower hillsides look like a green patchwork quilt from our height. Each little terrace was a patch of [a] different shade. We often don't wait for sunshine, but don raincoats and venture forth with umbrellas. We climbed to a height of 8000 feet a few days ago. ... I think one of the things I enjoy the most is looking at the gnarled old trees which have pushed their way through walls of rock. They are usually attired in gowns of soft green moss trimmed with fringes of delicate green ferns and silvery lichens.[40]

23
Mohandas Gandhi

On August 15, 1947, India discarded the British bonds that had shackled it for generations. Mohandas Gandhi, spiritual father of the nation, called the Indian Independence Bill "the noblest act of the British nation."[41] Still, Gandhi had no wish to lead India. That role would fall to Jawaharlal Nehru, who had long worked beside "Mahatma" for Indian independence. Lord Louis Mountbatten would fill the role of India's first governor-general. Mountbatten called Indian independence day "the most remarkable and inspiring day of my life."[42]

One might have forgiven the departing British, in the days and weeks after independence, for saying "I told you so." Within hours of the Independence Bill being signed, sectarian violence erupted across the country. As predicted, the Punjab province in the northern regions of India, adjacent to now Muslim-controlled Pakistan, was the scene of much of the strife. It is estimated that one million Sikhs, Hindus, and Muslims murdered each other during these dark days.

Over the next year, blood continued to be shed as Gandhi continued to preach non-violence. Despite several previous attempts on his life, no bodyguards separated him from the crowds that surged around him. One of those who approached was Mennonite Central Committee volunteer Vera Good.

> *I'd gone with a few friends to hear him speak. He always addressed the crowd seated on a charpai, a woven mat. Even today I can close my eyes and see him — a small, brown man who wore only a white wrap and sandals. I was close enough to him to see the wrinkles on his face. As large as the crowd was, [it] remained respectfully quiet as Gandhi spoke.*

And while Vera was unable to understand the Hindi message from "the great soul," the reverence of the crowd who listened could be understood in any language.

Yet not every Indian revered the Father of the Nation. On January 30, 1948, the day after Vera heard Gandhi speak, he was assassinated. Leading a prayer meeting, he was shot three times in the chest at close range. He spoke only two words before he died: "Hey Ram," meaning "Oh God." Mohandas Gandhi died within hours of the attack.[43]

Vera still has a vivid memory of the atmosphere in

the streets of New Delhi as the word of Gandhi's assassination spread.

> *The city went completely silent. It was deathly quiet as Indians learned that the father of their nation had been murdered. As we waited we knew that if it had been a Muslim who had ended Gandhi's life, then India would be torn apart.*
>
> *And ironically it was no Muslim, Sikh, or Parsi who'd fired the gun. Gandhi's assassin, Nathuram Godse, was a Hindu, like Gandhi himself. Godse represented those Hindus who felt that Gandhi had granted too many concessions to Muslims.*

After his death, Gandhi's body was cremated in a funeral pyre, and here the story becomes one of folklore. One tale tells that his ashes were divided and placed in a number of urns. These were passed on to his descendants as a memorial. Other reports dispute this and state that Gandhi's ashes remained in a bank vault until 1997. Then they were scattered over the holy waters of the Ganges River. Still other stories describe his ashes held for safekeeping by descendants until 2008, a full sixty years after the assassination, and then scattered across the Arabian Sea beyond Mumbai (Bombay).[44]

24

A Heartbreaking Decision

Over her three years in India, Vera had worked closely with her unit leader, Mr. Martin Schrag. During World War II, Schrag had worked in the Alternative Service program, placing American Mennonites in non-combat positions.

A capable administrator, Schrag soon came to rely on his efficient and resourceful office supervisor, Miss Vera Good. During their time together in India, Vera and Martin had become close friends. Given that they were both unmarried, it wasn't surprising that their working relationship would eventually become a personal one. But being so caught up in their present work, they talked little about their future – as two individuals or as a couple. Still, Vera says, "there was certainly an understanding between us."

A medical crisis would change all that. Vera recalls how "a friend, MCC nurse Mildred Shoemaker, and I were on a retreat when I discovered a lump in my abdomen. I asked Mildred to take a look at it. She did and thought I should see a doctor right away." Vera took her friend's advice and made an appointment with a physician. The diagnosis was an unsettling one. "There was a tumour growing in my abdomen and the doctor was convinced that it needed to be surgically removed immediately."

Vera pondered her next steps. "I could have returned home to Ontario to have the surgery, and there'd be no penalty for leaving before my term in India was up. Or I could trust the skills of an American surgeon working in India." It took little time to choose to have the surgery where she was at the time. She was shaken by the news that greeted her after surgery. "They'd had to do a full hysterectomy, and made sure I understood that this meant I couldn't bear children."

Vera's thoughts now turned to Martin Schrag. "I knew that he wanted to become a father someday. So I made the decision to set him free from any commitment that he'd had to me. 'This changes everything between us,' I told him. And he understood." It was a heart-wrenching decision for Vera. Over her long life, she has carried warm and loving thoughts of Martin Schrag with her.

25

A Bit of Fun
before Going Home

By the spring of 1949, Vera had started to contemplate what was next. Her three-year term in India ended late in September of the same year. "I was in my mid-thirties by now. And there was so much I wanted to do. But finishing my education was my first priority." She hadn't ruled out returning to India, either, at some point. "I would have liked to come back to teach but I knew that was probably unlikely. India was for Indians now."

On September 23, 1949, Vera said goodbye to colleagues who were remaining in India. She had made plans to do a bit of European touring before she returned to Canada. Martin Schrag and another colleague, Esther Book, whose commitments had concluded at the same time, would be along for the adventure, too.

The trio travelled by train out of India to Karachi

in the new nation of Pakistan. Governed by Muslims, Karachi was now a far different city than when Vera had briefly stopped there three years before. At Karachi, the friends boarded a boat that took them to Naples, Italy. From there they caught a train that would head north into Western Europe.

With stops in Italy, France, Austria, Switzerland, and Germany, the trio often found beds for the night thanks to a flourishing MCC European network. And then there was food! "We tasted pizza pie for the first time in Italy," recalls Vera. "Delicious!"

Germany was particularly unforgettable. Only four years after the war had ended, the country remained in shambles. "There was still so much destruction from Allied bombing," says Vera. "Rebuilding had begun, but it had a long way to go."

> *As we continued our travels, our eyes were opened to the human cost of war, too. Four years after peace was declared, there were still a large number of refugee camps. It really shocked us. Men, women, and children – sometimes as family, sometimes alone – were waiting to be admitted to countries like Canada and the U.S.*

The last leg of the tour saw the trio crossing the English Channel to the British Isles. Exploring London gave these North Americans a chance to witness the results of five years of war. "Rebuilding was going on throughout London, but many buildings were still rubble. It made us realize how hard hit England had been hit by Nazi bombing. "

By mid-December the friends were in Holland. There they boarded an ocean liner en route to New York. Vera has vivid memories of the Atlantic crossing. "I'd had an easy September crossing three years ago. It was a far different story than returning in December with high waves and fierce winds."

PART THREE

Vera Returns Home

(1949–1954)

26

An Unexpected Delay

Disappointment greeted the ship's passengers on docking in the port of New York. "We arrived on Christmas Day, but they wouldn't let us off the boat … [because] most staff at the dock were home with their families," Vera reports.

After saying goodbye the next day, the three friends went their separate ways – Martin Schrag and Esther Book to the west and south; Vera to the north, by train. It was surely an emotional parting between Vera and second man she had loved. "Where would his life lead him?" she wondered. "Where would my own?"

Boarding the train in New York City, Vera disembarked in Hamilton, Ontario. She was met there by several members of her family. With a laugh, Vera recalls her sisters' reaction when they first set their eyes on her. "I didn't have a winter coat when I left India, so I took one out of a bin of discarded clothes that had been sent from North America. Why anyone would send a winter coat to India is a mystery!" Vera had judged the coat serviceable, if perhaps a bit on the short side. "I had no idea what the styles were at home." Minutes after greeting her family, she got a lesson in 1949-era fashion. "My sisters were pretty horrified with the coat and told me to return it to recycling – right away!"

From Hamilton, the Goods crowded into brother Milton's car and headed for Kitchener-Waterloo. Tired and disoriented, Vera was still very happy to be home.

Over Vera's final months in India, she had been weighing her options for when she was settled at home. One saw her attending Goshen Mennonite College in Elkhart, Indiana, to take her Bachelor of Arts degree. A return to India to teach also tantalized her. "I made some inquires to see if there was any chance of this. The answer I got was, 'Next to none. Indians don't want foreigners there.'" So by default, Vera set her sights on Goshen. She would have to work for a while, though, to pay her tuition and board. "I returned home from my sightseeing tour pretty poor."

Brother Milton came to the rescue. He had become Office Manager of Boehmer's Heating and Building Supplies of Kitchener. Given his younger sister's credentials and character, Milton knew she would be an asset in Boehmer's main office. And so he offered her job. A few months of living at home and earning a paycheque would see Vera Goshen-bound in September of 1950.

27
At Goshen

Founded in 1894, Goshen College filled the niche of a Christian liberal arts college in the American midwest. Students interested in careers in teaching or nursing could also register with Goshen's Faculty of Education or its Nursing School. The latter faculty ran in coordination with the city hospital in nearby Elkhart.[45]

While the majority of Goshen's student body was American Mennonite, this was not a prerequisite for admission. Students from a variety of faiths across Europe, Asia, and Africa flocked to Goshen, as well as a number of Canadians. Certain key Mennonite values were integral to Goshen's curriculum. Pre-eminent was its Christian-centred learning. This encompassed both pacifist beliefs and stewardship/service to others. The college's motto of "Culture for Service" guided Goshen – in the classroom and in the dormitories.[46]

Vera stepped off the train at Elkhart and was met by her elder sister Viola. Viola had been at Goshen since 1936, having left Waterloo to take an undergraduate degree there. Viola had surely benefitted from the opportunity given to her of a college education. By the time Vera arrived to begin her own Bachelor of Arts studies in September 1950, Viola had completed her undergraduate degree and had gone on to take a master's degree at Northwestern University in Evanston, Illinois.

In the coming years, Viola Good would also take graduate courses in personnel at Columbia University in New York City. This would eventually lead her to become Goshen's Dean of Women, where she would remain until her retirement at age sixty-five.

In Goshen, Vera rented a room close to the college campus and settled into the business of school. She calls her first few weeks "a bit of an adjustment." "I was now thirty-five years of age and I hadn't been a student since 1943, when I was at Stratford Normal School." She admits that her age pegged her as a bit of an "outsider." And while Vera enjoyed taking classes once again, she admits that she was under-challenged intellectually. "Only philosophy gave me some trouble. That kind of abstract thinking took some work." She adds with a laugh, "Or maybe it was just me not being a very philosophical person."

On the other hand, her early childhood education

classes were delightful. "One day a baby was brought into the class for us to observe developmentally. We all loved that." The interaction with babies must have tugged at Vera's heart. "I had always seen myself as being a mother one day." Vera's medical problems in India precluded that possibility.

As graduation from Goshen approached in spring of 1953, Vera again contemplated her next step. She now held a Bachelor of Education degree in sociology, but viewed that accomplishment as only a stepping stone to more education. "I wasn't done with school. I wanted to go further." "Further" was attaining a Master of Education degree, which she decided to pursue in the United States, at Northwestern University in Evanston, Illinois, rather than in her native Ontario. "It was really Viola who encouraged me to do my MA in the U.S. I hadn't yet decided if I was going to remain in the U.S. or go back home; she felt that taking a graduate degree in the States was helping me cover my bases."

Then Goshen's President Miller threw a monkey wrench into Vera's plans. Miller also served as a member of MCC's Executive Board of Governors, and in this capacity he invited Vera to work for MCC as their Treasurer of the Board in India. "It was an honour and even a wee bit tempting, as I hadn't ruled out returning to India. But my vision saw me teaching children there, not crunching numbers."

Torn, she asked President Miller what he would say to his own sister if she was facing a similar choice.

"He said to me: 'If it was my sister, I'd say don't take it. You'll spend your days in an office pushing a pen.'" Having had considerable real-life experience in an office setting during her years at Kaufman and a shorter stint at Boehmer's, Vera didn't need any further encouragement to make up her mind. "I thanked him, but said no to India."

Instead she would return to Ontario. Her plan to begin a master's degree was dependent on having enough money. She would have to get a teaching job to afford the tuition.

28
Making It Work

Vera's plan saw her doing master's degree courses during summer sessions over several years. But this plan would only work if she got a full-time teaching job with a convenient two-month summer recess. And the position would need to be in Ontario, where she was certified to teach: "It would be ideal if I found a job around the Waterloo area where I could live at home, but really, I'd take pretty well any job that was offered."

As usual, Vera was selling herself short. In the Ontario of the 1950s, a precious few teachers, especially those in elementary schools, held a university degree. Vera Good, BA, would surely be considered a prize by most Ontario school boards.

After sending a rash of application letters, Vera waited for responses. And come they did, but surprisingly, not from her home Waterloo County. "I was quite disappointed with that," she recalls. In the end, she accepted an offer to teach with the London School Board.

Her placement would be at the brand new North Brae Public School in the northeast section of the rapidly growing city. Vera's responsibility would be a grade 5/6 class.

> *I was delighted about this but nervous, too, because I had a request to make before I accepted. My Northwestern course was a full nine weeks long and it started in mid-June. So I'd not quite be able to finish the school year. I'd need to leave two weeks before the end of term. Of course I wouldn't expect to be paid for those two weeks.*

No doubt delighted with the jewel they'd found in Miss Vera Good, the London Board readily agreed.

And so in the spring of 1953, Vera said good-bye to Viola and Goshen and headed straight to Northwestern. After summer term ended in late August, she would return home to Ontario. Enough time to get her classroom in order.

29
Revolutionary Educational Concepts

Northwestern University's roots went back to 1850.[47] Seventeen years before Canada became a nation, a group of nine American visionaries gathered to begin planning a university north of the present-day city of Chicago. These forward thinkers envisioned a seat of higher learning that would serve the (then) Northwest Territory of the United States of America.

In 1853 they purchased a 379-acre tract of land twelve miles north of the bustling midwestern town, and soon the shovels were in the ground. In due time, a settlement began to grow and was christened Evanston, in honour of one of the founding fathers, John Evans. Classes began in 1855, with two faculty members and ten students.

By the time Vera Good arrived on campus in 1953, Northwestern had become one of the most respected postsecondary institutions in the United States. The university's teacher education program, where Vera was enrolled in part-time MA studies, was considered among the best in the country.

From the outset, Vera loved what she was learning. While officially registered in a Master of Arts program, her timetable was peppered with education courses. Over the coming summer, Vera's view of teaching would be enriched through courses in educational philosophy, educational practice, and teaching the gifted child.

Vera's arrival at Northwestern coincided with the dawn of the "Discovery method" of educational philosophy.[48] Influenced by the American psychologist Jerome Bruner, proponents of this method were led by the belief that all children have a natural curiosity and desire to learn. It is only if material becomes difficult for the individual child's stage of development that the learner will become bored. Interest in learning will be stimulated when the material is presented at the level of the child's development.[49]

Inherent in the Discovery method is the role the teacher plays in the learning process. The traditional teacher-led, teacher-centred (Socratic) methods of instruction are not conducive to optimal learning. Learning must be student-centred; learning must happen through self-discovery. Accordingly, students interact with the world by exploring and manipulating objects, wrestling with questions and controversies. In the Discovery approach, the school library is as important a setting for learning as the classroom.

It was a keen Vera Good who packed her books and suitcase after classes ended and headed north to Waterloo. She planned to spend a short time visiting with family before moving to London. She had found a boarding house there to her liking, and she would be driving her first car.

30
Back in the Classroom

Soon after her arrival at North Brae in 1952, Vera took the occasion to speak to her new principal, in order to gauge his reaction to some of the ideas she hoped to bring into her classroom – primarily the Discovery method of learning.

> *I was sorely let down by his response. He didn't encourage me in the slightest – in fact, he didn't seem that much interested in any of my thoughts about the Discovery method and student-centred learning. Instead, he instructed me to concentrate on following the curriculum ... and that was the extent of it.*

In retrospect, Vera takes responsibility for not lobbying her administrator to take her ideas seriously. "In situations like this I didn't push – that was part of my character. When I was rebuffed, I just accepted it. And in the end, that didn't get me anywhere."

Still, in fairness to her principal, Vera acknowledges that he was facing other pressing issues at the beginning of a school year. North Brae, built in a rapidly growing subdivision in the northeast section of London, welcomed new students virtually every day. This reflected a steady stream of young families moving into the area and enrolling their children in the neighbourhood school.

The student explosion caused headaches for both North Brae administration and its staff – Vera Good included. "I started off the year with a grade 5/6 class. Then a few months later, I was re-assigned to a different grade, then a third time over that first year. It was a terrible way to start."

To make the situation more problematic, resources were in short supply. "Books for reading and doing research were pretty well nonexistent." And given that books were at the core of self-directed learning and the Discovery method, Vera soon grew frustrated. "So on Saturday mornings, on my own time and on my own expense, I picked up those students who wanted to read books and I drove them to the London Public Library."

By the new year of 1953, with no indication that the status quo would change at North Brae, Vera had decided to look to another board of education for employment. "I'd heard excellent reports about the progressive attitudes in Etobicoke, west of Toronto, and I decided to apply [there]." London's loss was certainly Etobicoke's gain. The Township of Etobicoke Board of

Education surely saw a gem in Vera Good and hired her to teach for the 1953–54 year.[50] She would be placed at West Glen Public School in the rapidly growing area west of the city of Toronto.

Etobicoke Board records place Vera's salary at $3100 per year. Vera's extra qualifications, a Bachelor of Arts degree at a time when the vast majority of teachers only had senior matriculation (grade 13) and a year of Normal School, surely put her a step up from other teachers of similar teaching experience. They would earn between $2200 and $2900 per annum.[51]

The Board readily allowed its new employee to cut the school term two weeks short. As had been the case the summer before, Vera was committed to returning to Northwestern to continue her MA studies. And so in mid-June, Vera said goodbye to North Brae Public School and headed south to Illinois. "I had faith that my next year at West Glen was going to be a much more rewarding one."

31

New Concepts,
New School Board

At Northwestern, Vera had enrolled in a graduate course that focused on the gifted learner in the classroom. Giftedness was a relatively new concept in the teaching world and was controversial among educators. Vera soon became a convert to the responsibilities that the education system had to the very bright student in the classroom. She describes the attitudes of the time:

> *Teachers really didn't think much about "the gifted learner." I guess we were conditioned to focus our attention on kids who struggled academically, kids who needed help. If a child was clearly advanced, he or she was just accelerated to the next grade.*

Over the summer, Vera had opportunity to visit several model gifted classrooms in Evanston. "They inspired me, and I couldn't wait to have the opportunity to put into practice what I was learning."

Inspiration led to unbridled enthusiasm – a state of mind that overshadowed Vera's usual reticence. Not yet a practising teacher with the Etobicoke Board, she composed a letter to Etobicoke's Deputy Director of Education Lloyd Smith. (Smith had been on the interviewing team who had hired her to teach in Etobicoke.) "I told Lloyd Smith what I was learning at Northwestern and shared some of the ideas that I was picking up. I said that I hoped that I'd be able to be able to use some of these teaching techniques in the fall in my own classroom." Little could Vera have anticipated how, in the months to come, this letter would alter the course of her teaching career.

Vera's own innovations began even before her class of grade 5/6 students at West Glen Public School returned to school in September. She rearranged their desks out of the traditional rows into circles of learning. Then she wasted no time in implementing the "Discovery and Reporting" teaching approach. The philosophy lent itself beautifully to teaching science. Vera shares a lesson in the teaching of volume – the Discovery way.

Instead of presenting a perplexing formula, the

teacher moves the students into groups. Then she gives each group a small pail of water sitting in an empty bigger tub. Students are instructed to add marbles to the small tub of water, watching how much overflows into the empty tub.

This amount of water is then measured. The volume of displaced water is equal to the volume of the object that was submerged. Out of this discovery, the principal of the displacement of water is understood.

History lessons were ripe for the Discovery method, too.

I had my students role-playing, in costume, the Fathers of Confederation meeting in Charlottetown, Prince Edward Island, as the politicians carved out the creation of the country of Canada. The kids got involved in the characters they were playing and began to understand the magnitude of what the men had been deciding – the building of a country! It was a great learning experience for them – much more enlightening than a boring Socratic lecture on the Charlottetown Conference.

The Discovery method wasn't complete without the reporting step of the process. After a Discovery lesson, individuals in the group would report on what had gone on in the activity and what they had learned.

"The reporting step was key in fixing the lesson in the student's memory," states Vera.

Not all of Vera's colleagues were impressed by the new teacher's novel approaches to learning.

> *The teacher whose classroom was next door to mine thought my class was far too noisy. One day I had some of them out in the hallways doing a certain activity and she roared out of hers to scold them. "You must be from room 13 [Vera's classroom]," she scolded my students, "because nobody else makes that much noise."*

In the early spring of 1954, Vera's principal called her into his office. He advised her that the next day, Etobicoke Director of Education Dr. Ken Preuter and Deputy Director Lloyd Smith would be coming to see her teach. Why, he wouldn't – or couldn't – say. Vera was assured enough of her abilities to ward off undue nervousness about her superiors' visit. But the unconventionality of what they would be seeing left her somewhat apprehensive.

> *I always started off each day by turning the class over to one of my students. He or she would take us through morning announcements. I'd sit or stand with the students while the "teacher" led the activities. When I had a question for the "teacher," I raised my hand like the other students. So that's what*

Preuter and Smith were going to see when they visited my class.

The next day, the esteemed visitors welcomed and seated, Vera proceeded with opening exercises as she did each morning. Other than the occasional grin from the administrators, they revealed nothing on their faces. Sometime after control of the class returned to Teacher Good, Preuter and Smith silently left. From the smiles on their faces, it was clear they had enjoyed the experience.

Vera spent little time contemplating the reason for the supervisors' visit, or what comments had come from watching her lesson. Managing a classroom of twenty-five excited youngsters left little time for woolgathering.

Some weeks later, Vera took a phone call at school from Director Preuter. He got right to the business of his call. "He was offering me the position of principal of the newly completed Queen's Court Elementary School." If she accepted, she would be the school's first administrator.

"I was shocked," Vera remembers. "After all, I'd been with the Board less than a year." Still, she was delighted and accepted the offer. Vera jokes about possible reasons for her appointment.

The schools were exploding at the seams, with dozens of new ones opening up. Boards of education across

*the province were scrambling to find principals to
lead the schools. I guess that's why they decided to
take a chance on me – a woman – as a school administrator. They didn't have enough qualified men!*

In accepting Dr. Preuter's offer, Vera Good be-
came the second woman principal in the Township of
Etobicoke school system – and one of only a handful in
Ontario.

Having accepted the post, Vera turned her
thoughts to the anticipated response to her promotion from her colleagues. "I'd only taught for one year
in Etobicoke. And now I was being named a school
principal? I wondered what other teachers would think
about this." She had little time to ponder. Days later,
she was on her way back to Northwestern University to
complete her MA program.

**Henry & Mary Good
(c. 1905)**

Photo: Nancy Silcox

**The Good Family (L-R): Loreena, Edna, Milt, Viola,
Erma, Vera, Robert, & Harold. (date unknown)**

Photo: Nancy Silcox

**Vera Good (top center) with her 1946 class at Riverbank School (outside
of Breslau, just east of Kitchener, Ontario). She taught at the one-room
schoolhouse for two years from 1944-1946.** *Photo: Nancy Silcox*

Vera Good in India. (c. 1947)

Photo: Nancy Silcox

Vera Good in her 30s.

Photo: Nancy Silcox

Vera upon her graduation at Goshen College.

Photo: Nancy Silcox

Vera's first Principalship at Kipling Grove Public School in Etobicoke, Ontario. (c. 1955)

Photo: Nancy Silcox

Just Married: Vera Good and Talleck Nowakowski. (1971)

Photo: Nancy Silcox

Dr. Vera Good in the 1980s.

Photo: Nancy Silcox

**Photos from the set of the renowned TVO children's show "Polka Dot Door."
Dr. Vera Good served as executive producer and educational consultant during the development and inception of the show.**

Photographs by Jed MacKay.
Digital images courtesy of Travis Doucette/ Retrobox Media / www.retroboxmedia.com/

Dr. Vera poses with a plush toy of Polkaroo, one of the characters on "Polka Dot Door."

Photo: Nancy Silcox

Dr. Vera Good in 2000.

Photo: Nancy Silcox

PART FOUR

Board
Administration

(1954–1960)

32

Queen's Court Elementary School

Vera wasted no time after her return to Etobicoke from Northwestern University in organizing her new school. Queen's Court Elementary School was located in what Vera termed "a working-class area of Etobicoke," where a number of immigrant families had settled. The new principal soon learned what school boosters new Canadians were. "There were very few problems with either the students or with their parents. Mom and Dad just wanted their children to succeed in a new country, and they were very cooperative with the school."

One of Vera's first administrative duties was to build a strong link between school and community. The Home and School organization was an integral forum for achieving this goal. Home and School meetings became events where both board and school announcements were publicized, as well as where parental input was sought. Principals could expect disgruntled parents to air their grievances in these high-profile public meetings.

In those days, principals were also expected to teach. And so Principal Vera Good would spend one period each day with a grade 8 class. As "head teacher," she was continually looking for opportunities to encourage her teaching staff to use some of the innovative teaching strategies that continued to percolate south of the border.

But this rookie principal was a realist, too, and knew full well that new teaching methods and concepts would be a bitter pill for some teachers to swallow. "A few, at least, were just stuck in the old way – with the teacher as the expert at the front of the class, and all knowledge coming from him or her." Even so, as she approached the end of the school year, Vera was satisfied, even encouraged that she had made some inroads with the more progressive-thinking of her staff. And she looked forward to the trend continuing over the next school year.

Then the unexpected came with a phone call. "Director Preuter informed me that I was needed next year to open up another new school. So I'd be transferred there for next September." Vera guesses that the board had her pegged as a "starter." There was another surprise in the call. Preuter also asked her to begin setting up a program for gifted children in the Etobicoke Board. Vera laughs: "I guess I'd let myself in for this with that letter to Deputy Director Lloyd Smith during my first year at Northwestern."

Youthful, enthusiastic, and energetic, Vera took the call in her stride. In later years, the revolving assignments would weigh more heavily.

33
Vera Multi-Tasks

Even with the pressure of starting yet another new school in September, as well as laying the foundations for a new board initiative, Vera, as was her custom, had no plans to let a summer pass without taking university courses. And so, late June saw her heading stateside. But instead of the slower midwest pace of Evanston, Illinois, she'd be in the thick of bustling New York City.

Columbia University would be her home away from home for the months of July and August 1955. With the lofty reputation of being on the cutting edge of educational thought in North America, Columbia offered part-time, summer master's and doctoral courses to accommodate practising teachers.

Vera could hardly count the hours till she was a student again. "I wanted to take as many courses in education as I could – pedagogy, values education, educational theory – and I wanted to absorb as much as I could." Vera emphasizes that even though she was taking doctoral level courses, she was not at this point formally pursuing a PhD. "I was taking the courses because they interested me," she explains. From conversations with her Director of Education, she felt he was supportive of her goals too. "When I told him where I'd be over the summer, he gave me his blessing."

Director Preuter surely had infinite faith in Principal Vera Good, even with only two years of administrative experience behind her. And well he should – it was a rare school principal who could be immersed in graduate studies work all summer and then be organized and ready to open a new school come September.

And then, of course, there was that little extra assignment called "gifted education." In retrospect, Vera is matter of fact about the heavy responsibilities she took on at this time of her life.

Well, you know, I just did it. There was no question that I had too much to do and couldn't manage it. Remember I'd taught eight grades, over thirty students, in one classroom at one time. The assignment I had now was far easier. I had a teaching staff who would look after the students while I did the planning work!

The moment Vera returned from New York, she dove headfirst into getting her new school shipshape. Located in an upscale area of Etobicoke, then a pleasant country drive from the hustle and bustle of metropolitan Toronto, the brand new Kipling Grove Public School showed Principal Good a different face than had Queen's Court. "Kipling Grove parents were generally more affluent than those at Queen's Court. They were no less supportive, but they asked a lot more questions both of my teachers and of me."

In Vera's spare time, she began to lay the foundations for what would become one of Ontario's earliest and most respected programs for gifted children. Planning, with Vera in the leadership role, would take place over the school year of 1956–57, in preparation for offering the new program in 1957–58. At the time she had no idea who would be in charge when it was up and running. "I was doing the preliminary work but whether I'd be running it, teaching in it, or continuing as a school principal was yet to be discovered."

Vera's first priority would be to gather a committee of like-minded teachers around her. They would then move on to the mechanics of identifying the students who would be invited into the program. This screening process would begin in regular classrooms across Etobicoke. Classroom teachers would nominate students whom they felt would benefit from gifted programming. Parental permission was essential at this stage. The next step would see the nominated students undergoing an assessment supervised by a fully qualified psychologist. A standardized intelligence test called the WISC – the Wechsler Intelligence Scale for Children – was used to formally identify those students who presented as gifted or above average in intelligence. Any student who scored 120 IQ and above would be considered for the program.

And if there was any time (or energy) left in Vera's working day, as a principal she was expected to attend and take part in a number of administrative committees and workshops. They ran the gamut from budget to curriculum implementation, from new Department of Education initiatives to student attendance. Committee meetings were also an opportunity for principals to gauge the mindset of their peers with regard to the changes and initiatives that were rolling out regularly from the Ontario Department of Education.

A quick study, Vera readily ascertained who was in the "fast lane" of educational thought and who favoured retaining the status quo. Some, like Vera herself, were urging their teachers to move out of their comfort zones and into the "Discovery and Reporting" models of learning. Then there were the "leave it be" educators, lagging behind.

These get-togethers also allowed Vera to measure her own performance among her peers. More than sixty years later, she reflects on her own presence in these high-level gatherings of leadership.

> *These types of meetings showed me at my least comfortable – at my least confident. I wanted to contribute my thoughts and ideas, and I had many, but I usually held back. I think I was afraid that they'd be discounted by my peers. Of course they were all men, except myself and one other female principal. So I tended to listen more than share.*

Vera calls her reticence to contribute vocally "a lack of self-confidence." "I think it had a lot to do with my Mennonite upbringing – more likely to remain in the background." Eventually, Vera laments, "I found out that this trait didn't help me professionally."

By the end of her first year as Principal of Kipling Grove Public School, Vera was given next year's marching orders. "I was being offered the full-time principalship of the Gifted Program for next year." She was of two minds about the invitation.

> *I was of course flattered and enthusiastic to be on the ground floor of a brand new educational program.*

But I hadn't had the opportunity to spend more than one year in any school or assignment. I'd spent one year in London, one in West Glen, one at Queen's Court, and now one at Kipling Grove.

"So," Vera adds, "I'd never had the opportunity to learn and grow in any of my positions." And now the men who made the decisions about everything were moving her again!

Still, gifted education was an exciting new field, and Vera agreed to take on the role of principal. However, she would have to burn the midnight oil, since as usual she was leaving for the United States to continue her coursework at Columbia University. This gal was an old pro at multi-tasking, though.

34
Etobicoke's Gifted Program

As the Etobicoke Board of Education took the beginning steps of implementing programming for its gifted students, it looked south of the border for guidance. Educational resources and programming differed from state to state, but the gifted student in the American school system had been studied since the early 1920s.

America's first School for the Gifted, in Worcester, Massachusetts, opened in 1901.[52] Fifteen years later, in 1916, Lewis Terman, considered the father of gifted education in the United States, began his longitudinal study of 1500 exceptional children. Four years later Terman published his groundbreaking results in the book Genetic Studies in Genius.[53]

In his studies, Terman uncovered a number of measurable differences between gifted and the "average" learners. In addition to their superiority in academic subjects, bright children were "slightly better physically and emotionally in comparison to [what Terman called] "'normal students.'" So too were these "brainiacs" "emotionally more stable" when compared to "normal students," found Terman. For the majority of those identified, Terman judged that they were "most successful when education and family values were held in high regard by the student's families."[54]

In Canada, programming for gifted students lagged dismally behind that in the United States. Canadian educational researcher Samuel Laycock, in his publication "Trends in the Education of the Gifted in Canada," discussed the climate for exceptionally bright students in Canada of the 1950s:

Being identified as gifted was seen as a negative and a nuisance to the educational order. Parents and society put greater emphasis on the importance of popularity, conformity and athletic prowess than that of high academic achievement. It was due to these facts that, unless also excelling in athletics, gifted children were rejected and alienated by their peers.[55]

By 1957, in Etobicoke at least, the status quo was about to change. Vera Good would be leading the charge in recognizing the rights of the gifted learner in the school system. Etobicoke would join only four other school boards across Canada in implementing a Gifted Program.[56]

Kipling Grove was designated as the first congregated school for gifted students in the Etobicoke Board. Busses would transport students to Kipling Grove from their home schools across the board catchment area, and later return them there. Three classes would run: grade 3/4, grade 5/6, and grade 7/8.

Vera initially had some concerns about the social aspects for students in these congregated classrooms. "I wasn't sure how they would like being pulled out of their home schools – how they'd like being away from their usual school friends." She was pleased that her concerns were largely unfounded. "Most of them loved their classes and adapted easily to being in a new program, being in a new school, and making new friends." But not everyone – within the education system and outside it – was a fan of gifted education, says Vera.

It remained a controversial discipline – with teachers, with administrators, with parents, and with the general public. In fact in these early years, programming for the gifted was a hard sell. Every day someone would say to me: "Bright kids have it made. Why would they need any more attention or all these resources?"

In response to such critics, Vera would remind them of the long-range benefits of gifted education:

I'd usually remind those who questioned that our society depends on the brightest minds to lead us — politically, scientifically, medically, and otherwise. These potential leaders need to be encouraged and stimulated to achieve their potential. It is essential that our school system set these children free — by challenging them to be the best they can be.

Despite the skeptics, Vera hosted a steady stream of visitors from across the province to see one of Ontario's first gifted classes in action. In years to come, Vera would be roundly praised throughout the Province of Ontario for her expertise and her support for gifted children. Her response to these tributes is customarily modest.

My main contribution to gifted education, I believe, was promoting the Discovery approach to learning. In my thoughts, this was the bottom line for programming. Our classes encouraged students to identify their interests and develop the research skills

to discover everything they wanted to know about
[those interests].

It would be a full ten years after Vera Good's
Gifted Program was initiated that the publication of
the Hall-Dennis Report, *Living and Learning* (1968),
jump-started more boards of education to initiate
programs for gifted students.[57] Guided by the United
Nations Universal Declaration of Human Rights, the
Hall-Dennis Report set out several fundamental ideas.

What principles, then, should govern our consider-
ations and guide us to conclusions and recommen-
dations? We may with faith and reliance turn to
The Universal Declaration of Human Rights of the
United Nations for assistance. Regarding education,
Article 26 of the Declaration says:

"1. EVERYONE HAS THE RIGHT TO EDUCA-
TION. EDUCATION SHALL BE FREE, AT LEAST IN
THE ELEMENTARY AND FUNDAMENTAL STAGES.
ELEMENTARY EDUCATION SHALL BE COMPULSO-
RY. TECHNICAL AND PROFESSIONAL EDUCATION
SHALL BE MADE GENERALLY AVAILABLE AND

HIGHER EDUCATION SHALL BE EQUALLY ACCES-
SIBLE TO ALL ON THE BASIS OF MERIT."

"2. EDUCATION SHALL BE DIRECTED
TO THE FULL DEVELOPMENT OF THE HUMAN
PERSONALITY AND TO THE STRENGTHENING OF
RESPECT FOR HUMAN RIGHTS AND FUNDAMEN-
TAL FREEDOMS. IT SHALL PROMOTE UNDER-
STANDING, TOLERANCE AND FRIENDSHIP AMONG
ALL NATIONS, RACIAL OR RELIGIOUS GROUPS,
AND SHALL FURTHER THE ACTIVITIES OF THE
UNITED NATIONS FOR THE MAINTENANCE OF
PEACE."

"3. PARENTS HAVE A PRIOR RIGHT TO
CHOOSE THE KIND OF EDUCATION THAT SHALL
BE GIVEN TO THEIR CHILDREN."

*With these we accept the concept that every child in
Ontario is entitled, as of right, to the opportunity
of access to the educational and training facilities
for which his talents qualify him; that no condition
of race, religion, language, or background shall be
allowed to impede his progress to full citizenship in
all its plenitude.*[58]

In discussing the broad talent range of the gifted
learner, the Hall-Dennis Report observed that

*it must be recognized that there are many children
who have special gifts in music or art or drama,
but who have no particular interest in the sciences
or mathematics or other academic disciplines. The
curriculum must provide for their progress and for
graduation with emphasis in their specialties. These
children cannot be branded as failures by the fact
that their talents lie in special areas rather than in
the traditional disciplines.[59]*

Serving the needs of gifted children? Why, Vera
Good had been on this bandwagon since 1953!

PART FIVE

Down a Parallel Path

(1958–1962)

35

A "Break"

After two years as Principal of Gifted Education for the Township of Etobicoke Board of Education, Vera decided to resign.

> *I'd been invited to join the Faculty of Education at Goshen College, and the invitation piqued my interest. After all, since the time I was a child, I'd wanted to be a "teacher of teachers," and I was finally getting my chance to fulfill a lifelong dream. I felt, "How could I turn such an opportunity down?"*

But there were more factors playing out in Vera's professional life that urged her to take a break.

> *I was feeling some doubts about remaining in the Gifted Program. I'd given up my role as a school principal to get it up and running. And while I was called the principal of the program, I didn't always*

feel that the two positions were parallel. I wasn't sure that I hadn't taken a step backwards in administration in taking on the role.

Vera also wondered how much more she had to offer the program: "Maybe it was time for another person to take it from there."

Vera's natural curiosity and her dedication to the Discovery method also played a role in her taking up Goshen's offer. "I was always tempted by new horizons, and this was an opportunity to get more directly involved in pre-service teacher education." In choosing to resign rather than ask for a leave of absence from her school board, she would be free to explore further opportunities in the United States, if she so wished.

Vera vividly recalls telling her superior, Etobicoke Director of Education Dr. Ken Preuter, her news. "He was surprised and disappointed but wished me luck – reminding me that I was always welcome to come back to Etobicoke." Years later, she wryly laughs at her director's promise. "Welcome back to what? I should have asked at the time. Another big mistake I made."

Vera's Etobicoke colleagues held a big send-off party for her. "Despite all the kind words and people saying 'we'll miss you,' I was sure that I'd done the best thing for me." Bigger adventures were on the horizon.

36
Goshen Again

The opportunity to be in close contact with her oldest sister, Viola, had been high on Vera's list of Goshen attractions, too.

Viola had played a very important role in my life, especially in the early years of my life, and I was eternally grateful to her. It was because of Viola that I was allowed to carry on to high school after my year at home. My other sisters hadn't had that privilege. And because of her I'd had a chance at a different sort of life.

So, piling clothes, books, and other necessities into her car, Vera once again headed south, across the border and toward the state of Indiana. "I really had no preconceived notions of how long I'd be at Goshen," she admits. "My contract was open-ended – I could leave after a year or stay for ten." She rented modest accommodation close to the college.

Viola welcomed her "little sister" to Goshen and apologized to her that she couldn't give her accommodation – even for a short-term stay. Vera explains Viola's living situation:

> She'd been the Dean for Women at Goshen – a high academic position – for years and years. But for reasons I couldn't understand, she still lived in a small apartment in Kulp Hall, the women's dormitory where she'd worked as Matron in the early years. I thought it was past time, at age fifty-one, that she move on.

With one of Viola's friends, Vera convinced her sister to buy a lot near the college and build a house. Vera drew up the plans for a duplex and it was soon under construction. Appealing to Viola's frugal side, one side of the residence was for her to occupy; the other side was to rent out. It was thanks to this project that Vera discovered that she had a talent for design. Vera Good the architect would lie dormant for over thirty years before she came to life again.

Vera found considerable professional satisfaction in teaching at Goshen College. One of the courses she instructed in the Faculty of Education was Classroom Management. Surviving for two years in a one-room schoolhouse had surely qualified Vera in this area of expertise.

She had also been charged with the responsibility of designing and supervising a kindergarten class as part of the Faculty of Education program. It seems Vera's reputation as a start-up expert had travelled south of the border, too! The kindergarten would be housed right on the Goshen campus, with pre-schoolers drawn from the neighbourhood as well as from Goshen staff.

Paramount in Vera's program structure would be incorporating new approaches to education for these littlest of learners. The Discovery method of teaching was as relevant to four-year-olds as it was to teenagers. Vera made sure that all teachers hired to work with the Goshen kindergarten took in-service training in the most recent philosophies in teaching and learning.

37
New York City

Two years slipped by like a short Canadian summer, and it was decision time again for Vera. Big decision time. Stay at Goshen? Look for another teaching job in the United States? Or return to Ontario? Then she began to think in another direction.

> *I was already in the U.S., not all that far from Columbia University in New York City, where I'd been taking part-time courses for a couple of years – for fun, for interest. I'd never thought before about directing them toward an official Doctorate in Education (EdD) Maybe I should now.*

There was a small catch, though. "I'd been taking courses in the summer time, but I'd need to do a full-time residency period on the Columbia campus to complete my doctorate."

Why would Vera, a Canadian with a Canadian

teaching certificate, elect to do a doctorate at an American university? "Even in the early 1960s, Canada offered almost no opportunities to take a Doctorate in Education," Vera explains.[60] "So the U.S. was way ahead of Canada in this regard."

Her length of stay at Columbia would depend on how quickly she could complete all her requirements. Coursework, written exams, orals, a directed work period, and settling on her dissertation would take at least a year, maybe longer. But the timing seemed right: "There was nothing calling me back to Ontario, so I decided to stay."

Always frugal with her money, Vera had saved much of her income from teaching at Goshen College. "So I felt I could afford the expense." She moved into a dormitory close to the large Columbia University campus, then met with her faculty advisor to plot out her direction. Within hours of her arrival, Vera got down to the business of being a student again.

> At age forty-five, I was older than many of my classmates but it didn't seem to make any difference to me or to any of them, it seemed. We were all there – with different ages, different backgrounds, from different countries – for the same reason. So it wasn't hard to fit in at all.

New York City was a place where Vera could take advantage of cultural opportunities as well. "I liked living there. There were people from all around the world and there was so much to do – seeing plays, concerts, ballets, and all within walking distance." Vera counts her time in New York City as happy and fulfilled.

One of Vera's degree requirements saw her doing research at several New York City public schools. With a partner, John McGinnis, also a Canadian, she assessed the district's reading programs. The study focused on a wide range of variables: What materials were teachers using? What were the strengths and the weaknesses of the particular reading programs? And what rate of success were the teachers seeing in their students?

When she wasn't analyzing results of the reading study, Vera's nose was to the grindstone, working on her dissertation. "It was a bit of a dreary topic," she admits – "Supervision and Curriculum Development." Once the dissertation was complete, she would need to defend it before a panel of Columbia professors and supervisors.

With her courses and research work scheduled to be completed in late summer of 1962, she was free to return to the working world. And so the "where to" question raised its beguiling head again.

38
Big Decisions

During Vera's Columbia sojourn, she had come to some conclusions about where to continue her professional life. "I'd decided that I'd rather work in Canada's educational system than in the U.S. And I liked what I was hearing education-wise north of the border."

What she was hearing was growth and innovation. Over the close to four years of Vera's residency in the United States, Ontario's population and economy had blossomed. With this came the increased need to better educate youngsters to take their place in a booming province. Despite this economic progress, the dropout rate in Ontario high schools remained high. If the province aimed to take a prominent place in the economy of tomorrow, that exodus from schools needed to be addressed.

The Robarts Plan aimed to do just that. In an auspicious speech delivered to the Ontario Legislature by Premier John P. Robarts on April 3, 1962, the face

of education in Ontario was forever changed.[61] Under
the Robarts Plan, Ontario secondary schools would
henceforth be streamed into three academic divisions:
Basic, General, or Advanced levels. In their grade 8 year,
students would be counselled by teachers as to which
academic stream would offer them the best chance of
success.

A progressive thinker, Dr. Vera Good, still in
her academic perch at Columbia University, had ap-
plauded these measures and felt she wanted to be a part
of the Ontario education revolution. But how? Where?
Should she return to an Ontario Public Board of Education? Should she seek employment at a university? Or
at a teacher's college? She certainly now had the qualifications to do the latter two.

> *So I decided I'd shop around a bit. I'd see what was
> out there for me and what I'd be best suited to do.
> I reasoned that the logical place to start was at the
> Etobicoke Board of Education. This was the employ-
> er that had treated me so well, that had promoted
> me and had showed faith in my abilities by promot-
> ing me.*

While Vera was not specifically looking to be
promoted to Superintendent of Education – the top of
the Ontario school board hierarchy – she does admit
to wanting a position where she could influence board
policies for the betterment of the students. "I hoped

that my track record would invite the Board to offer a position where I could offer real leadership, where I could share in the exciting changes that were happening in education." Would she have been satisfied with a Superintendent of Education position had it been presented to her? "Yes, I would have," she answers. "Or a parallel position."

And so, Vera placed a call to her former Director of Education, Dr. Kenneth Preuter. "I told him that I was planning on coming back to Ontario and wondered, if I did return to Etobicoke, what position he could offer me." During a congenial dialogue, Director Preuter proposed that Vera take a job as Head of Instructional Services. "It was a position of considerable responsibility, equal to a Superintendent, he told me." Director Preuter also assured Vera that the job, if she should take it, was a step up from an elementary school principal and principal of Etobicoke's Gifted Program.

Everything in Vera's country-stock background, as well as her previous experiences with the Etobicoke Board of Education, influenced her to take the Director at his word. "I saw no need to search further. I trusted that I'd be treated well by him and the Board – as I had before I left for Goshen in 1958."

Looking back on that particular day, on that particular conversation, Vera calls her acceptance of Director Kenneth Preuter's offer "the biggest mistake of my life." "It was the wrong decision; it was a bad decision and I paid dearly for it. I wish I'd chosen differently."

PART SIX

Inspector's Business

(1962–1964)

39
What Have I Done?

When Vera Good returned to the Township of Etobicoke Board of Education in August of 1962, she carried with her a prestigious academic title. She was now a Doctor of Education, a degree equal to that of a PhD and earned from a prestigious American university. Vera was undoubtedly one of the few administrators with the Board – man or woman – who held such a degree.

Not that Vera flaunted her achievements in the least. Schooled by her Mennonite roots and upbringing, Dr. Vera Good presented as the modest, understated, and self-effacing woman she was. "I wanted my work to speak for me, not my academic qualifications." And anyway, degrees weren't the important thing. Education was, and she was champing at the bit to get down to work, as soon as she discovered what she would be responsible for. That information would come when she arrived at her new job, no doubt.

Warmed by the "welcome backs" of her colleagues at the Etobicoke Board, Vera felt a certain disappointment as she looked around the workplace.

> *Four years after I left, the board administration was still dominated by men. And while there were some female learning consultants – especially in areas like primary education, music, and perhaps physical education, I was the only woman in upper administration. And that troubled me.*

Personal disappointment was added in the days and weeks to come. "Basically, I had no idea what I was supposed to be doing as 'Head of Instructional Services.' There was no job description, no itemization of duties, no list of staff who would answer to me." Neither was there any indication where she fit into the administrative chain of command.

A quick study, Vera realized that despite her "lofty" promotion, the office hierarchy was still exactly as it had been when she departed in 1958: Director of Education Preuter at the top of the totem pole, Deputy Director Lloyd Smith as second in command, and the superintendents under them. "And I fit in nowhere," Vera concluded. Thinking back to those days, Vera is at a loss to recall what filled her working hours. "I didn't do much; I'd run the occasional workshop and keep track of the subject consultants. What else, I have no idea. I honestly can't remember how I filled the work day."

Time at hand inevitably led to brooding on the situation she found herself in. "I couldn't understand why Preuter had hired me back only to put me in the awful, useless position I was in." Vera could think of only one rationale for the about-face.

> *I think he hadn't gauged his superintendents' attitude about having a woman equal in responsibility to them , making decisions at the highest level of the Board. And after he and I had spoken on the phone, he must have told his gang the position that he had given me and they were angry. They said no, they wouldn't agree to me being on the same level as themselves.*

And so, Vera speculates, while the Director of Education couldn't withdraw his offer, he could water down her responsibilities. Vera looks back on this dark period of her professional life as "useless days, useless weeks, and useless months. I was just miserable."

Frustrated and depressed by the situation in which she found herself, Vera also placed blame for her situation on herself.

> *I had accepted this role on faith. I hadn't asked Preuter the hard questions that I should have when we talked on the phone. I hadn't insisted that he outline my role. I should have requested that he*

state – in writing – key points like: "What are my duties?" "What are my decision-making prerogatives?" "Who will I report to?" and "Who will report to me?" It was up to me and me alone to ask these hard questions. And I didn't.

The traditional role of women in Mennonite culture may also help account for Vera's actions. "Being aggressive and demanding wasn't part of my Mennonite upbringing. And in the role I'd carved out for myself as an adult female, this became my weakness."

Insult was added to injury when later in the year an announcement came from the Director of Education that a new superintendent had been hired. And that the Head of Instructional Services would report to *him*! This latest slap in the face thoroughly tested Vera's belief in her own abilities. "When you're out of step, as I seemed to be, you begin to doubt yourself. Maybe I wasn't any good; maybe I wasn't up to the job. Maybe that's why I'd been bypassed."

As Vera's second year in purgatory brought no change in her situation, she knew she would need to regain control of what had become an untenable situation. "I decided that the time had come for me to look outside Etobicoke for administrative positions elsewhere." She applied to various Toronto and area school boards to develop their Gifted Programs and waited eagerly for responses. When they didn't come, Vera became suspicious.

While of course I could never prove it, I am almost certain that my Director of Education had something to do with my not even being given a call back. Before contacting me for an interview, the other boards would have asked him for a reference. And I'm guessing he gave me a bad one, because I never heard from any of them.

Some time later, Vera was summoned to the Director's office. "He was furious with me, charging that I had 'the audacity' to apply for other jobs. 'After all I've done for you,' were his words." Decades later, the memory of this interview still causes Vera pain. "He didn't want me, but he was going to make sure that nobody else would hire me." Not usually given to metaphoric turn of phrase, Vera finds an apt figure of speech: "Preuter pretty well wiped the floor with me."

In time and with considerable insight, Vera came to an understanding of the "why" of this period of her life. "I don't believe it was wholly personal; it was more that I was a woman and I had worked myself up to being in a man's world. And they weren't ready to accept someone like me yet."

And despite her troubles with the Etobicoke Board of Education, Vera still had cause for celebration. In 1965, she successfully defended her doctoral thesis. She also wrote her Inspector of Education papers, which would qualify her for a position with the Ontario Department of Education. Thankfully, she did not have long to wait. In June of 1965, Dr. Vera Good handed her resignation to her Director of Education. She had been offered and had accepted a position as an Inspector with the Department of Education. And the reaction of Director Preuter, when he learned of Vera's new role? "It's too bad you had to take a demotion," he commented.

40
The School Inspector

In his 1893 report, "The Education System of the Province of Ontario," John Millar, BA, Deputy Minister of Education for the Province of Ontario, laid out the awesome powers of the school inspector:

The Inspector while officially visiting a school has supreme authority in the school and has the right to direct teachers and pupils in regard to any or all of the exercises of the school room … He is at liberty to give such advice to pupils or to the teacher as he may deem necessary. All his counsels, however, should be given in the spirit of kindness and his authority should be exercised not with a view to over-awe or intimidate but to reform abuses, correct mistakes, and inspire confidence and respect. He should be courteous and considerate and when reproof is necessary it should be tempered with gentleness and sympathy.[62]

Twenty-five years after Millar's report, little of the aura surrounding the omnipotent school inspector had faded – at least in Vera's memory as a little girl attending a country school.

> *Our teacher would tell us that we had to be especially good because THE INSPECTOR was coming to our classroom. And we were terrified. Was he inspecting us? For bad behaviour? For rudeness? For being stupid? For not knowing the answer to our teacher's questions? For forgetting our lunch box? For being messy in our notebooks? Would we be sent home? Would we be kicked out of school?*

What Vera's teacher, the stoic Miss Hallman, would not have divulged to her Bearinger School students was that the school inspector had come to judge *her* – her pedagogy, the appearance of her classroom, the behaviour of her students, even the cleanliness of the environment. A bad inspection could see the teacher removed from the classroom and blacklisted from employment in that particular school district. A positive inspection would guarantee a job until she married or looked for an income above the poverty line.

The next time Vera entertained the school inspector was in 1943, in front of her own classes at Riverbank School.

> *My students of course were as terrified as I had been*

as a little girl. But I was quite calm. It might have been more stressful if the inspector had been someone other than Mr. Dobrint. He'd been my Stratford Normal School Master and the one who had recommended me for the Riverside teaching position before I'd even graduated.

Inspector Dobrint's report on teacher Vera Good was glowing.

And now, Dr. Vera Good was a school inspector herself. In accepting the appointment she notched a place in history, becoming the first woman to be appointed to an inspector's position with Ontario's Department of Education.

Save for the duty of inspecting teachers, one which Ontario's school inspectors carried out once, twice if time permitted, in the beginning teacher's first year in the classroom,[63] Vera's role in 1965 would be considerably more far-reaching than it had been when she had been inspected twenty years previously. Charged with the duty to "co-operate with school boards to the end that the schools may best serve the needs of the pupils,"[64] inspectors now had duties outside the classroom as well. Approving grants to boards of education, liaising with principals, monitoring new school construction, fielding media inquiries, and facilitating professional development opportunities for teachers also filled the school inspector's days. And if there was any time left, keeping abreast of the latest education developments in other Canadian provinces and beyond – especially in the United States – provided food for thought.[65]

41

The Supervision Division

Vera soon learned that she would be an inspector in the Supervision Division of the Department of Education. Other inspectors worked in Program, Curriculum, or Professional Development. Some were specialized program inspectors overseeing Technology and Trades, or Special Schools and Services for the Blind and Deaf.[66] From memory, she calls up a job description that outlined her duty to "supervise and assess the educational program carried out in the public, separate, and secondary schools of the province of Ontario." The scope of responsibilities brings on a laugh: "Oh, if we had any time left we were to 'maintain constant contact with schools and teachers.'"

Following on the heels of Vera's division placement, she learned that she'd be working out of the Department of Education office in Waterloo. In recent years, the Department had made moves to decentralize and had created ten branch offices across Ontario.

Waterloo was the location of Midwestern Office #5.[67]

"So I'd be moving back to Waterloo," says Vera. The prospect of returning home after almost two decades away wasn't greatly appealing.

> *I had a lovely apartment in Toronto, but I knew that finding something comparable in little Waterloo would be impossible. And it was. I finally located an apartment building that was under construction, due to be ready by later winter. So I grabbed it.*

Fortunately her brother Milton and his wife Verna had room in their Waterloo house, and they would be glad to make their home Vera's headquarters until hers was ready. Even so, "Living with my older brother for months … it wasn't an option I would have chosen for myself."

On the office front, Vera would share duties with six male colleagues. These "field inspectors" would be assigned to liaise with public elementary, separate, and secondary schools in Waterloo, Grey, Perth, Wellington, Brant, Norfolk, and Oxford Counties.[68] "So if you didn't like driving, then you were in the wrong job," Vera advises. Waterloo #5 Field Inspectors would report to Area Supervisor R.A. Barnhold, who took his marching orders from the Department of Education offices in Toronto. In most cases, requests for a field inspector to deal with an issue in any one of the schools came through Supervisor Barnhold.[69]

Vera's gender was not her only distinction among her colleagues. She alone held a doctoral degree. Her area of specialty was listed as K–8 social studies. Her colleague K.W. Kenney, MEd, was assigned to supervise K–8 mathematics. The other five inspectors, each with specific subject specialties, liaised with secondary schools. The division of labour is a telling one. In my own home county, Oxford, circa 1965, five secondary schools were located in the county's three urban centres. Elementary schools must have numbered at least 100 across the county. Inspectors Good and Kenney were certainly kept hopping!

And then there were students designated as needing Special Education.[70] Acknowledging that certain students had physical, emotional, and intellectual needs outside the regular curriculum, Ontario's Department of Education added Special Education supervision to the list of duties of the Ontario School Inspector. In 1965, school inspectors made 446 visits to Special Education classes; they "worked with" and "referred for assistance" 141 of those students, and undertook "assessments" of a number of them.[71] "Working with staff" to ensure their special students' needs was a part of the school inspector's job description as well. Surely none of these highly placed educational bureaucrats had time for wool-gathering.

In August 1964, Vera packed her suitcases, boxed up her books and papers, returned the key to her beloved Toronto apartment, and headed to Waterloo.

Given the record of her past employments, she wondered: "Who knows how long I'd be there?"

42
Learning the Ropes

It took Vera little time to realize the magnitude of the job she'd taken on in Waterloo. "It was a huge responsibility, and it would take several years for me to become familiar with it and feel comfortable." And given the revolution in education that was going on around her, Vera knew "the rules" could change from one day to the next.

The 1960s had ushered in unparalleled changes in Ontario's education system. The Robarts Plan of 1962 (see chapter 38) had seen a thorough overhaul of Ontario's secondary school system. On the heels of the Robarts overhaul came the announcement by incumbent Minister of Education William Davis that Ontario's high school graduates would now have more education choices than work or university. The Province of Ontario was set to open a number of community colleges.[72]

And there was more to come. *Living and Learning: The Report of the Provincial Committee on Aims and*

Objectives of Education in the Schools of Ontario – popularly known as the Hall-Dennis Report of 1968 (discussed more fully in chapter 34) – proposed to forever banish teacher-oriented instruction, focusing instead on child-centred techniques. Memory work was to be replaced with an emphasis on Discovery method learning.

For Vera, there was nothing particularly new or revolutionary in the Hall-Dennis Report:

> *I'd become a convert to child-centred teaching when I was taking courses at Northwestern University in 1952. I'd brought the Discovery method of teaching to my students in both London and Etobicoke in the 1950s. Child-centred learning was what guided me when I started the Gifted Program.*

As a school inspector, Vera's responsibilities were nothing if not varied. Observing new teachers trying for their permanent contracts topped her list of duties. Not every probationary teacher made the grade. Sexual misconduct, poor classroom management, reports of out-of-school "unteacher-like" behaviour such as alcoholism, drug use, or family violence would be cause to dismiss a teacher. Former Waterloo County Board School Inspector Howard Parliament calls up a memory from the mid-1960s of an elementary teacher being dismissed for a homosexual liaison. "This teacher was counselled to leave teaching," reports Parliament.[73]

Sharing Department of Education initiatives with principals' groups was also high on Inspector Vera Good's duties. On occasion, she might be called upon to meet with parent associations. "Driving out of town, often in the evening, was the norm in the job," Vera reports. As the province's one-room schools like Bearinger and Riverbank were closed in the mid-1960s and students moved to amalgamated schools,[74] inspectors were also on the front line of parent and community concerns.

There was fun on the job, too – at least school inspector-ly fun. One of Vera's favourite roles saw her leading teacher workshops on new philosophies in education. "I liked giving practical assistance in the classroom too. But the best times – they didn't happen nearly often enough – were when I could teach children. I really missed that and wished I could get back to teaching."

43

"Not Again"

As the calendar indicated that spring was indeed coming, even in notoriously snowy Waterloo, Vera gave thought to the job she had taken on.

As my first year as an inspector of schools was draw-ing to a close, I felt that I had only scratched the surface of learning what I'd begun to see as a mam-moth job. And learning the job was over and above the conditions we worked under — travelling from school to school, from county to county, in all sorts of weather.

Then there was the huge scope of our respon-sibilities. We dealt with everything from disciplin-ing teachers to meeting with community groups; from lobbying for a new school to passing on new directives from the Department [of Education]. It was truly overwhelming. I felt that I could be in the position for five years and still not feel entirely comfortable.

Vera's mood lightened considerably when her new Waterloo apartment was finished in March, and she could be on her own again. Things seemed to be looking up. Little could Vera have guessed that for her, March winds and April showers would bring more than May flowers.

A Department of Education meeting had taken Vera to Sarnia in late April 1964. Sarnia was a long drive and she was tired. Committee meetings had never seen Vera at her best. "I tended to listen more than I shared at meetings. The same reticence I'd had as a principal was still with me as an inspector." Vera always shone brighter when she was sharing ideas with teachers and encouraging students to discover the world around them.

It was with some surprise that she was called to the telephone during the Sarnia meeting. "I wondered who on earth it could be. The only one who knew my schedule was Barnhold, and he would have only interrupted me if it was an emergency of some sort." She took the call with some trepidation.

The caller was Dorothy Dunn, a Department

of Education official in Toronto. Fifty years later, the words Vera heard that day still ring clear.

> *"Vera, it's Dorothy Dunn here. You're being called back to Toronto – for a special assignment. Education Minister Bill Davis just announced in the Legislature that educational TV will be up and running in a year. And we need you here to work on it. You're to get yourself down to Toronto immediately."*

Vera was thunderstruck. 'I remember saying to her: 'I can't come now. Barnhold has me working on a number of projects here in Waterloo.'" Dunn's answer was clear: "Forget what Barnhold wants you for – you're needed more here!" The words over the phone came to Vera in a jumble: "I told [Dorothy Dunn] I knew nothing about television but she dismissed this and told me I was expected at the Department offices on Monday. I left the meeting in a daze."

On the drive back to Waterloo, Vera had time to reflect and take stock of her situation: "I'd gone through musical schools before in Etobicoke. And here I was again. Less than a year into the job and I was being yanked out once more because I was needed." By the time Vera arrived home, her mood was decidedly foul. "I was fuming. Did I have any control over my life? Apparently not. I was again leaving a job that I'd hardly had time to know – in a role where I felt I'd really achieved very little." Then there were the living accommodations: "I'd lived with Milton and Verna for eight months and I'd been settled in my new Waterloo apartment for only two months. And now I'd have to go looking for another apartment in Toronto."

Sleep barely visited Vera that night. In the morning she touched base with Supervisor Barnhold, gave her apartment superintendent the news that she'd be leaving, and packed her bags. She would arrange to have the rest of her belongings shipped at a later date. Vera admits that as she headed east along the 401 highway, "I was in no positive frame of mind as I neared Toronto."

PART SEVEN

"What Do I Know about Television?"

(1965–1981)

44
Bill Davis's Big Announcement

On June 2, 1965, Ontario Education Minister (and future Premier) William G. Davis rose in the Ontario Legislature to deliver a portentous announcement.

> *The Ontario Department of Education intends therefore to apply to the Board of Broadcast Governors for a license to establish a television broadcasting system for the purpose of producing and transmitting programs of educational nature.*

And if this pronouncement hadn't caught the attention of any dozing legislators, his timeline did.

> *… we expect to begin transmission in Metropolitan Toronto and the surrounding area on the ultra-high frequency Channel 19 within one year of the date of approval. Service to educational institutions will begin soon after.*[75]

Davis noted that the newly named Educational Television (ETV) would initially purchase air time from the CBC.[76]

Anticipating criticisms that viewers in more isolated reaches of the province would once again be deprived of services available to residents in metropolitan areas, Minister Davis promised that within two years, educational television would have thirty-four stations covering 95 percent of the province.

Addressing the matter of staffing the new initiative, Davis forged on:

> *The provincial educational television staff members concerned with program ... will be selected largely from the educational profession and branches of the media and those already involved in curriculum development in the Department of Education.*[77]

Had she been able to peer into a crystal ball, Ontario Inspector of Schools Vera Good, presently shuttling between schools in Woodstock, Hanover, and Brantford, would surely have been surprised to see that one of those "television staff members" would be herself.

45

The Staff Arrive

Bill Davis had several people in mind to play the lead role in tackling the educational TV behemoth. Ran Ide, former Superintendent of Secondary Schools with the Sault Ste. Marie Board of Education, was one of them.

In his book *The Transparent Blackboard*, Ide recalls the moment he was buttonholed by Bill Davis's Deputy Education Minister Zach Phimister about assuming the role of TVO Chairman.

> *He informed me that the Minister had decided to have educational television in Ontario. Then in a tone that that seemed to imply that he did not think much of the idea, he added that they were looking for someone to take charge of this initiative ... that they had only been able to identify three people and the other two had turned it down. So I had twenty-*

four hours to decide whether to take the job.[78]

Later, Ide must surely have questioned his sanity as he took stock of the assets he had at hand. "We had the use of only two offices in the Department's complex … virtually no staff, no airtime and no programs."[79]

No matter these daunting details, Ran Ide took on the challenge and had his work cut out for himself. While offices, airtime, and programs might be cobbled together in an abbreviated period of time, finding staff to produce quality programs would be a Herculean task. "People with talent, creativity and commitment were the most critical element in the equation. And they were difficult, but not impossible to find."[80]

In an early meeting to identify educators who might fill the bill, Dr. Vera Good's name was suggested. It took Ide little time to realize the gem he had uncovered.

> *I learned that Vera had her Doctorate in Education from Columbia University. She had also worked for four years [sic] in India in food distribution to the poor and impoverished, and had a very special feeling for the disadvantaged.*

> *On the other side of the coin she had initiated the first program for gifted children in the Toronto area at the request of the Etobicoke Board of Education.*[81]

Clearly dazzled by Vera's past accomplishments, Ide describes his prize catch as "a brilliant and progressive teacher who brought with her tremendous energy and academic qualifications."[82]

Vera's ahead-of-the-curve pedagogy was where Ide knew she would bring innovation to the table in television programming. "Vera was aware of the inadequacies of current approaches to individualized and diversified learning experiences. She felt changes were needed to cope with the explosion of knowledge and the ever-increasing complexity of society."[83] "Progressive" was the operative word in Ran Ide's books.

Working with Vera on the ground floor would be Jack Ross, previously the Head of Personnel in the Department of Education, and Leo Lacroix, a former school principal and board of education superintendent. Lacroix was a francophone and would be invaluable in setting up French-language service in the province.

Vera herself would fill the role of Executive Producer of Children's Programming. Her wide-ranging position would see her supervising the development of programs that would focus on child development and education. She would also be responsible for conveying the wonders of educational television to boards of education and teachers across the province. This was a task that would come to try her severely.[84]

Under these few pioneer television executives, a number of teachers, principals, school and board administrators, as well as technicians and support staff, would work around the clock to get educational TV off the ground. "Pretty well anyone who they felt could do the job – as impossible as it seemed – was buttonholed," offers Vera. "And it seemed we had no choice to refuse." Clearly Vera's "farm girl" work ethic would stand her in good stead over these early days.

46
"A Carte Blanche Approach"

Despite a shortage of staff, Vera and her team enjoyed a carte blanche approach to early programming for children. "We had no superiors hanging over our shoulders saying 'Yes that's great,' or 'No it's terrible – get rid of it.'" The trial-and-error approach was standard fare for Vera and her crew in these early days.

Ironically, the first programs that came out of the backrooms of TVO under Executive Producer Vera Good weren't for children at all. "They were intended primarily for teachers," says Vera, "to help educate them on a wide variety of children's issues that they'd see in their classrooms."

Programs such as *A Different Understanding* were produced under Vera's watch. The half-hour series was developed to assist teachers in identifying and understanding various learning styles. Each week a new episode of *A Different Understanding* was presented. Titles included "What Do You Do with a Kid Like That?"

"The Invisible Handicap," "Tag Along," and "I Was a Kid Who Couldn't and Now I Can." The series covered such topics as learning disabilities, autism, giftedness, and attention deficit disorder.

To advise on these programs, Special Education experts, including classroom teachers, were brought on board. One was Babs Church. TVO Chairman Ran Ide highly respected Church's abilities and knew she would work well under Vera Good. "Babs was able to impart a special understanding of the unique problems by both the handicapped and the gifted as they faced the problem of growing up and becoming adjusted to the customs and mores of our society," said Ide.[85] Another indispensable staff member reporting to Vera was Christa Singer. Her background included a specialty in the effects of divorce on children, as well as adoption, teenage suicides, and reform schools.

An integral part of Vera's role was heading up TVO's Teacher Education Branch. An oversize job in itself, this entailed connecting teachers of Ontario with educational television. Ran Ide recalls Vera's skepticism as she turned her sights to selling educational television to reluctant teachers. "It was a challenge to educators to see if this apparently passive activity of watching television could be successfully integrated into the teaching–learning process."[86] The attitude of the rank-and-file teacher bordered on fear in these early days. "Teachers saw educational TV as taking away their jobs, and in most cases they wanted nothing to do with it," says

Vera.

Vera's plan would eventually assuage those fears. It saw five TVO vans stationed across the province in Thunder Bay, Sudbury, Ottawa, London, and Toronto. Each van was equipped with miniature TV production systems, including VCRs (called VTRs then), monitors, overhead projectors, and cumbersome, heavy televisions sets. The vans also included a technician and a teacher educator. While Vera didn't accompany her roving "ambassadors," she kept in constant touch with them via telephone.

Vera's methods saw the TVO van staff inviting themselves to various school board offices and schools to show off what educational television had to offer. Normal Schools, churning out newly minted young teachers, were on the list too. After a dazzling "show-and-tell" session, discussion groups and question-and-answer periods were facilitated by TVO staff. Vera also anticipated teachers' criticism that using television as a teaching tool without follow-up material wouldn't make the grade. To this end, she and her team put together educational kits that teachers could use with the various programs.

Despite these initiatives, issues well out of Vera's control stood in the way of early educational TV acceptance. Lack of televisions in the schools was at the front of the line. Retired Waterloo Region School Board teacher and principal Louis Silcox, teaching at a Waterloo rural school in 1971, describes the status quo regarding technological equipment of the day.

> *At our school there were a couple of TVs kept in a storage room. Great big clunky monsters on rolling stands. There was no such thing as a media technician in the schools then, so if the TV went on the "fritz" you waited for days till somebody from the board office came out to fix it. Teachers were on the honour system and were supposed to record – ahead of time – the day and time of booking out the TV.*

The best-laid plans …

> *Even when you booked the TV well ahead, there was never any guarantee the equipment would be where it was supposed to be. On a whim, somebody might have decided to treat his or her students to a television program. And out went the TV, and who knows who had it?[87]*

Despite the difficulties, young teachers like Louis Silcox were more than ready to embrace technology. A favourite program with both this teacher and his grade 4/5 students was *Moon Vigil*, an interactive TVO science series. Host Warner Troyer took his student audiences to the moon, where they filed reports on their discoveries. Another winner for Silcox's science class was *The World of BJ Vibes*. Here students were introduced to the physics of sound.

As TVO writing staff became more comfortable with the fine points of writing for TV audiences, the quality of shows improved markedly. Eventually most high schools hired audiovisual technicians to supervise TV and other technological equipment. In many elementary schools the burden was foisted on the school librarian.

47

First Programs
for Pre-schoolers

Their feet now thoroughly wet in programming for teachers and school resource staff, Vera Good and her staff now focused on developing programs for pre-schoolers. Ran Ide praises Vera and her staff in this respect.

> *This helps to explain a very special interest at ... TVOntario in the development of programming for the very young. The hope of course was that if we could devise appropriate programs for children we would be able to make a positive difference in their chances for success when they began formal schooling. Fortunately we had the ideal person on staff in Vera Good.*[88]

The educational philosophies behind TVO programming for pre-schoolers had their grounding in

Vera Good's pedagogical beliefs, forged first at Northwestern University and later at Columbia. "Child-centred learning – discovery and sharing – continued to guide me in the role I'd taken on in educational TV. We wanted our programs for young children to broaden and enrich their lives." To this end, she encouraged her production staff to use a "free-floating approach." "We were experimenting and learning, laying down foundations of the excellent programming that would come later."

Ontario children didn't have to wait long to experience that "excellent programming." By 1968, the wheels were turning in Vera's fertile brain for what would become TVO's benchmark series for little ones – *Polka Dot Door*.

With the blessings of boss Ran Ide, Vera set out on a fact-finding mission to the BBC studios in London, England. There the popular British series *Play School* was produced. Vera liked what she saw in London and picked up some valuable advice.

> *The Play School people suggested that because of kids' short attention spans, the programs should be done in brief segments. Multiple hosts rather than regulars were advised, too. This would avoid children*

becoming too attached to one television "friend" who might leave the series at some point.

Vera then headed to New York City. There she took notes on the Children's Television Workshop's hit series *Sesame Street*. Vera's reaction to *Sesame Street*'s Mr. Hooper and his friends Big Bird, Bert and Ernie, Grover, and the Cookie Monster was less positive than it had been to *Play School*. "*Sesame Street* emphasized the teaching of numbers and letters, which it did with a lot of panache," Vera recalls.

But we were looking in a different direction. We wanted to get kids out of their seats, moving, dancing, singing, and expressing themselves, instead of sitting passively. So the series needed to have "bounce," with lots of singing and dancing. But it also had to encourage kids to use their imagination and their sense of curiosity about the world around them.

Vera's reports and ensuing discussion with her writers led the TVO folk to purchasing the rights to the *Play School* series. The BBC had developed kits that it sold to various foreign networks in France, Germany, Italy, and Spain. The British assumed Canada's culture was enough like their own to use the same format. With this framework to guide Vera's team, it was full steam ahead.

48
Making It Their Own

In her role as Executive Producer of Children's Programming, Vera worked closely with a team who developed and built *Polka Dot Door*. Dr. Ada Schermann, a Professor of Child Studies at the University of Toronto, served as consultant on the series and gave the show its name. Peggy Liptrott filled the producer's shoes, and Ted Coneybeare held the position of educational consultant. A number of support staff played their part as well.

Running five days a week, the half-hour show featured one male and one female host. Cast for this key role changed regularly. Over its two-decades-long history, *Polka Dot Door* served as the debut of over fifty young actors.

A number of regular toy friends also joined in the fun. They included Marigold, Humpty, Dumpty, and Bear, Grandfather Clock, and the Storytime Mouse. All were silent, with their human friends interpreting for them: "What's that, Marigold?" "You did what, Bear?" Over *Polka Dot Door*'s half-hour slot, a fast-paced combination of music, short-film inserts, and animated features kept the action hopping.

An appearance by the Polkaroo – only on Thursdays – was always anticipated by the viewing audience. Part kangaroo, part moose, the Polkaroo was resplendent in vibrant yellow, red, and green polka-dot rompers. While the Polkaroo did speak, his vocabulary was limited to one word: "Polka-rooooooo." A measure of mystery surrounded the beast. He could only be seen by the female host, who welcomed him when the male host was occupied elsewhere. "The Polkaroo was here and I missed him again?" was the returning host's common lament. It took perceptive youngsters little time to catch the connection between one character leaving and the other appearing.

By the late 1970s, TVO ended their agreement with BBC's *Play School*, deciding to focus their resources on *Polka Dot Door* as a purely Canadian children's series. In contrast to the "wow factor" of American children's programs such as *Sesame Street*, *Polka Dot Door* was characterized by "a certain simpleness." In a 1984 interview with the *Globe and Mail*, Ted Coneybeare (who eventually became *Polka Dot Door*'s producer) had explained the low-key mood: "Deliberately the shows are not polished – there's a hesitation, a naturalness … they're designed especially for the child. Especially the child watching alone."[89] Coneybeare also praised the abilities of Polka Dot Door's props makers. "We had great props people who could build fabulous castles from Kleenex boxes, but we always made sure when the host did it looked more or less as it would if a child did it … We always tried to engage with our audience."[90]

Airing from 1971 to 1993, *Polka Dot Door* became TVO's longest running series, with 383 episodes. In 2000, Dr. Vera Good, as the show's original Executive Producer, won a Gemini Award for Best Pre-School Program or Series from the Academy of Canadian Cinema and Television.

49
Vera's Legacy

In 1973, Vera's official role with TVO grew into
Superintendent of Pre-School and Teacher Education
and Early Childhood. Ironically, in television she finally
was bestowed with the title that she had been denied by
the Etobicoke Board of Education. And while her work
became less hands-on and more administrative, she kept
her eye on the children's programs that were coming out
of TVO. "We were developing children's series non-
stop," notes Vera.

And excellent products they were. After-school or
early morning programs such as *Today's Special*, *Jeremy*,
Music Box, *The Little Prince*, *Timothy Pilgrim*, and *The
Green Forest* gave pre-schoolers and primary school
children quality children's programming. Programs for
older children such as *Write On* and *Math Patrol* com-
bined entertainment and education.

Vera's influence continued to be felt in producing
programs for the classroom. Shows such as *How* and

Child Life in Canada were popular with teachers and did much to dispel their early concerns that they would be declared redundant in favour of the little grey screen. Obviously teachers were still needed to shepherd the kids in understanding what they were seeing on the little grey screen. *How* followed two children, Vicki and David, as they observed the differences between babies and grown-ups – from human infants to adults, from kittens to cats, from seedlings to mature plants. *Child Life in Canada* was designed to assist children in grades 4 to 8 in understanding the way of life of several cultural groups they might have found in their schools or neighbourhoods.

And so, as the 1970s passed and the 1980s opened, educational television in Ontario was blooming and booming. But now in her mid-60s, Dr. Vera Good was a little ragged around the edges. "I just had far too much on my plate and far too much responsibility. The waters that I had to tread in were far too deep and the result was that I think I only did a so-so job."

Vera's superiors and the staff who worked with her would disagree with her self-assessment. Colleague Babs Church praised her leadership style: "As a boss she supported, guided and generously trusted me to do my job effectively. She was universally respected as an educator and as a human being."[91]

Eventually, Vera got some relief. "As more staff was hired, bits and pieces of my job were sliced off. It was a relief and allowed me to continue on." She laughs:

"But I continued to have a corner office." "Someone told me that in most large organizations the corner offices were reserved for the most important people!"

PART EIGHT

Love, Finally

(1 9 7 0 – 1 9 7 6)

50
Not Too Busy for Love

Work had always consumed most of Vera's hours – and her thoughts. "To the exclusion of most other things – including relationships," she confesses. "It seems that for most of my life, I had been a career woman – a teacher, a student, a school administrator, and an executive. I thought I was just far too busy to spend any time on much else."

Still, she hoped that one day she could meet the right man and marry. But Vera realized that the chances of that serendipity grew slimmer as she aged. "I was in my fifties, and was what I'd call 'retiring in personality.' It was difficult to ever have a hope of meeting someone suitable at that stage in your life unless you were the aggressive type of woman – which I wasn't." As time marched on, the prospect of being alone in her elder years left Vera doubtful that there were any benefits in remaining single. "Most of my friends were married, many had children, and here I was still alone."

Then one evening chance came to call. Vera had been invited to a dinner at the home of a TVO colleague. It would be a mixed group of television and educational folk, with a smattering of friends of the host. In the company was Antoni Nowakowski, known to his friends as "Talleck." A Polish immigrant to Canada in 1959, Talleck had been a mover and a shaker in the construction business in his native land when World War II broke out in 1939. Like countless other Polish business owners, Talleck watched helplessly while his livelihood was seized by foreign invaders. Fighting back against such oppression, he had joined the Polish underground, a network of patriotic Poles determined to banish the enemy from their beloved land.

With the end of the war and Germany's defeat, one master was merely exchanged for another. Poland now paid allegiance to the USSR. Antoni "Talleck" Nowakowski joined thousands of like-minded Poles vocally opposed to Communism. Talleck would languish in Communist Poland until 1959, when he was able to accumulate enough money to leave Poland. Even then, he had to do it on the sly, with a forged passport to get through the iron gates. With a mere $2 in his pocket, Talleck found himself in Toronto, Canada, living with a cousin who had left Poland before the war. He immediately signed up for English classes and gradually acclimatized to the Canadian way – its culture, its people, and its language.

When he met Vera Good in 1970, Talleck's

prospects had improved. He was now a proud Canadian citizen, living at a respectable rooming house and working in an art supply store. Like many Poles, he was a lover of art and had once owned several Old Master works. "Apparently at the beginning of the war, Talleck had taken the paintings out of their frames, rolled them up and had hidden them somewhere where the Germans couldn't find them. After the war they'd disappeared and he never saw them again."

As the two lone singles at the soiree the evening of their meeting, Talleck and Vera gravitated to each other. Two individuals of more different backgrounds and prospects could not have been imagined! Still, Vera was intrigued by the loquacious Pole. "Talleck was an impressive-looking man, five years older than me. He was quite intelligent and spoke Polish, Russian, German, and English." While he retained a strong Polish accent, Talleck's command of the English language was good. And he was confident to have his voice heard in social gatherings such as this.

"For one so new to Canadian culture, Talleck was outspoken and opinionated," says Vera. "But when I got to know him better I preferred to describe him as sensibly stubborn," she chuckles. When, that evening, he asked Vera if he could see her again, she said "yes."

51
Complicated Business

Over their growing relationship, Vera learned much more about her beau's past:

> He told me that he'd been married in a Catholic Church ceremony in Warsaw, Poland, before the war. But he and his wife ended their marriage soon after. But no records of their divorce or annulment had survived the chaos after the war. Records in a place like Warsaw had gone with the Germans arriving. But documents or no documents, Talleck considered himself to be unmarried.

Vera worried about introducing him to her conservative Mennonite family, but the occasion, when it came, passed uneventfully. "They had no strong reservations about him. After all, I was close to sixty," Vera reports. Still, she didn't discuss Talleck's complicated marital and political background with her relatives.

Lost documents were only one of the challenges to be overcome if the couple was to marry. "We certainly wouldn't be welcome to be married in a Mennonite church. And without Talleck's documents confirming his divorce, we couldn't marry in a Roman Catholic Church either." It was a conundrum, but Talleck had a plan. Talleck plan's usually worked out – somehow, says Vera, with a smile.

In anticipation of an impending marriage, the couple began to do some house hunting. There were some ground rules. "Talleck wouldn't abide us living in an apartment. He said the long hallways reminded him of a concentration camp. He'd lost more than one Polish friend at the camps."

Vera learned that a TVO colleague was planning on selling his house, located in the exclusive Rosedale district of Toronto. She and Talleck made arrangements to visit it. "It was lovely, but certainly bigger than we'd use, and it needed a lot of repairs." But Talleck loved the house and convinced Vera that he could do much of the handy work himself.

A bonus to the property was its separate second-floor apartment. "So Talleck suggested that we could have a boarder to help with the expenses." Vera was making a good salary and a real estate transaction fol-lowed. Shortly after, they advertised "apartment for rent" and a call came from an interested party. He wanted to see the property.

> *This very expensive car stopped out in front of the house and a tall, lean man got out and came to the door. He liked [the apartment] but asked if we could do a few renovations before he took it. They weren't big ones, just cosmetic, and he'd pay for them. But I recall that he especially wanted red wallpaper in the front hall!*

Vera had taken scant notice of the inquiring party, leaving that to Talleck. "I had no idea who he was until sometime later Talleck said to me: 'Our renter says his name is Gordon Lightfoot. Does that name mean any-thing to you? It doesn't to me.'" Over the coming weeks, one of Canada's most well-known celebrities and the former Polish Underground Resistance fighter Antoni Nowakowski got to know each other, during Lightfoot's frequent visits to 6 Rosedale Road.

But who was going to reside in the upper-floor flat with the startling red wallpaper? "Not Gordon Lightfoot himself," says Vera. "We heard everything – from his manager to his special lady friend." Vera's memories are dim about the identity of their boarder. "I was still working long days at TVO and really didn't pay too much attention to the upstairs apartment," says

Vera. "That was Talleck's territory." All Vera knew was that the rent was paid by Lightfoot and somebody else lived there.

52
Getting Married

Meanwhile, Talleck's sister Barbara in Poland was continuing to search for records that would prove that her brother was legally able to remarry. But with communication difficult between the Communist Bloc countries and North America, Talleck hoped that a personal meeting between them outside Poland might prove helpful. With that in mind, Vera took a six-week leave from TVO and they left for Europe.

> *We'd remain in West Germany, hoping that Barbara would get permission to meet us there. But we waited, and waited, and waited. With only a week of my holiday time remaining, Talleck finally received a letter from his sister saying that permission for her to travel to Germany had been denied. She was considered a security risk to flee.*

But all was not lost – Barbara had been given

leave to travel to Splitz, Yugoslavia. That country, too, was in the Eastern Bloc of nations controlled by the Soviet Union. With that news, Vera and Talleck rented a car and headed south.

At the eleventh hour, Barbara arrived in Splitz. It was an emotional meeting between brother and sister, who had not seen each other since Talleck fled Poland more than a dozen years before. Barbara's words of assurance regarding the legality of his divorce convinced both him and Vera that their marriage would be a legal one.

Wedding plans dominated conversation after their return to Canada. On August 18, 1971, before a small number of guests, Vera and Talleck married in the chapel of St. Michael's Roman Catholic Church in Toronto. Vera was fifty-six years of age; Talleck was sixty-three. The party of ten then returned to 6 Rosedale Road and dined on lobster.

Marriage suited Vera well. She and Talleck enjoyed the rich cultural life that Toronto had to offer and regularly attended concerts and symphony performances. When warm weather came, Vera would pack a picnic lunch and they would escape the city for the clean air of the country. With a large Polish community in Toronto, there were frequent invitations to dinner. Vera felt at home in these gatherings. "Talleck's Polish friends always made me feel welcome and would speak English if I was in the party."

Talleck continued to work at the art supply store

221

until 1975, when he found himself in dispute with his superiors over a financial matter. Now in his mid-sixties, he decided to use the controversy as a reason to retire. That was fine with Vera. "He helped around the house, did some carpentry and renovating, and of course visited with friends."

Ongoing stomach problems in 1976 caused him to seek a doctor's advice. The news was devastating: "He had cancer of the stomach and the pancreas and there was really nothing medicine could do." When Antoni Nowakowski died on December 29, 1976, Vera was heartbroken. "We'd had such a short time together. He died far too soon."

PART NINE

Life after Love

(1976–2010)

53
What Does the Future Hold?

Work filled the holes in Vera's life after Talleck's death in 1976. And work there surely was at TVO. The 1970s had been a decade of significant growth for the network. Now on air an average fifteen hours a day, it had begun to broadcast in French in 1973. In 1974, one of TVO's most popular programs, *Saturday Night at the Movies*, with host Elwy Yost, aired. This was followed by TVO's first current affairs program, *The Education of Mike McManus*.

In 1981, at age sixty-six, Vera retired. Her stellar career as a pioneer in early educational television in Canada been preceded by scholarly and educational achievement, setting a high standard for women to follow. At her retirement party, Ran Ide spoke fondly of his first Executive Producer of Children's Programming, later Superintendent of Teacher Education and Early Childhood. "TVO owes much more than anybody realizes to Vera Good. There are a few people without whom the great experiment could never have succeeded and Vera was one of them."[92] And while Vera admitted that she would miss the fast-paced life of television production, she was ready to leave the ten-hour work days behind. "My work at TVO had been exciting and rewarding, with great creative people to work with. But I was tired – really tired – and I looked forward to taking it easier."

Sleeping in and afternoon bridge games would need to wait a while, though. Vera had accepted a short-term position from the governments of Belize and Jamaica to advise these countries on setting up educational television. Over the next two years, Vera travelled to the Caribbean several times with a technical expert from the CBC to advise communications staff there on setting up educational television. The work opened Vera's eyes to the huge communications gap between Canada and less technologically advanced nations. "It was really difficult to see how educational TV would be successful when the schools there were so technologically backward, with next to no equipment like televisions, VCRs, or even radios." She completed her consulting stint, feeling less than satisfied that educational television in those developing nations was much further along on a path to broadcasting than when she had arrived.

As she unpacked her bags and looked forward to real retirement, Vera admits to a feeling of trepidation. "Now what? ... The prospects ahead scared me. I wasn't prepared for retirement at all."

54
"I Wasn't At All Prepared"

Bridge, twice a week, filled some of Vera's hours, and there were always plays, musicals, and operas to enjoy in Toronto. Lunch out with friends with no need to rush back to work was delightful, too – if not hard on the waistline! Vera also did some volunteer work with the "Out of the Cold" program. But after decades of deadlines and assignments, her focus was now on fun and relaxation.

A member of Erb Street Mennonite Church in Waterloo until she moved to Toronto, Vera hadn't joined a church community during her years in the big city. Still, she enjoyed the feeling of peace and serenity that church offered and from time to time sampled various religious denominations. "I was a 'church tramp,'" she volunteers. "I attended this church and that one, as the spirit moved me." She had also found a travelling companion in her sister-in-law Jean, and the pair enjoyed trips to Russia, Australia, and Europe.

Still, five years after Talleck's death, Vera found

herself wondering if she was destined to spend the rest of her life as a widow. "I wasn't sure I wanted this; I felt that if the right person came along I'd be open to marry again." Little could she have guessed that she'd have a chance to explore this further in a trailer park!

Some years back, Vera's brother Robert and his wife, Jean, who made their home in Simcoe, had purchased a trailer which they kept at a trailer park in Lakeland, Florida. The Goods had made many friends there – most of them snowbirds like themselves. But Robert, a businessman, couldn't get away to the south as much as Jean could, and so Vera was invited to accompany her sister-in-law. One of the "Simcoe gang" was a retired farmer and widower named Scott Miller. A congenial and outgoing man, Scott was a regular at community barbecues, shuffleboard tournaments, and cards.

As Vera and Scott came to know each other, they realized they had commonality in their situation. "Both of us had lost spouses after long battles with cancer," explains Vera. And as their friendship deepened they came to discover another common ground. "Scott was having similar thoughts as I was about the prospect of being alone in the coming years."

Inevitably, the two began to discuss marriage. Scott was close to his three daughters Joan, Diane, and Judy, who lived in the Simcoe area. They were open to him marrying again. And in fact, a Miller–Good connection had already been made: Scott's daughter Joan was wife to Robert and Jean's son Paul.

By early 1985, Vera and Scott were planning a summer wedding. But there were some logistics that Vera would need to work out. They would surely live in Simcoe, where the family connection was strong, so Vera would need to sell her large Toronto home. That wasn't a problem, given its upscale location in the Rosedale section of the city. The house sold quickly and for a high price.

Vera Good and Scott Miller were married in August of 1985, at First Baptist Church in Simcoe. The reception for the small party – primarily Scott's family – was held at the Erie Beach Hotel in nearby Port Dover. The couple would live in Scott's Simcoe home while their new house on Oak Street was being built. This would give Vera an opportunity to fulfill a lifelong ambition – to design her own home.

> *Thirty years before, I'd drawn up the plans for Viola's duplex while I was teaching at Goshen. And I discovered I had a talent for it. Since that time, I'd always wanted to put my ideas into a house for myself. But up until this point, I'd always lived in apartments or houses other people had built. Now, I finally had the opportunity. I could hardly wait to see my ideas materialize.*

Before the hole was even dug in the ground, Vera was sketching!

55
"Obsessed"

As is her way, when any relationship or situation over her long life has gone wrong, Vera stoically shoulders her share of blame. And so she takes responsibility for her share of the problems that ensued between herself and Scott.

> *I became obsessed with the house. First with the planning and the building, then when it was up, with the decorating, both inside and out. I spent much of my waking hours researching, sketching, looking at paint and fabric samples, and on and on … That left Scott more or less on his own to find his own activities.*

Nor was Vera's house-planning regimen the only issue between the couple. Once married, they found the connection that had formed between them in a holiday setting was difficult to maintain in everyday life. "Scott and I had bonded in an artificial setting when we were on holiday. I don't think he and I realized how different we were from each other until we married."

Having lived in Chicago, New York City, and Toronto, and having held executive positions for most of her working life, Vera's interests were city-oriented. Scott, on the other hand, was well-established in his small-town community. Old friends, children, and grandchildren played a major role in his day-to-day life.

With the relationship at home strained, Scott spent considerable time at the homes of his three married daughters. After three years of marriage, in 1989 Vera Good and Scott Miller divorced. Vera remained in the couple's Oak Street home in Simcoe, with Scott moving to an apartment. He later bought a small home.

56
Transitions

After Vera and Scott divorced, Vera again took up a travelling life with Jean, now a widow. Robert Good had passed away in 1988.

Time at home in Simcoe revolved around twice-weekly bridge games, regular outings to theatre and concerts, and some volunteer work. Regular visits with her nephew Paul, his wife Joan and their children, with niece Marybeth Smith and her husband, David Smith, all living in Simcoe, as well as with nephew Jim Good and his wife, Eva, in London kept her family connections strong. "We always called Vera our favourite aunt," says Joan.

Retirement also brought honours for Dr. Vera Good. In 1990 she was inducted into the Waterloo County Hall of Fame. She recalls the phone call that informed her of her selection.

When the representative from the Hall of Fame said

*why she was calling, I told her I thought there had
been a mistake. "It's not me who should be inducted
but my brother Milton. He's the one who has done
so much good in Kitchener–Waterloo. He's been a
Waterloo County builder and has given so much for
his community. Not me!"*[93]

The call was not a mistake, and indeed later that
year Vera joined a distinguished group of Waterloo
County natives in receiving this honour.

By 1998, Vera felt she was at another crossroads in
her life. "My nieces and nephews had been the reasons
I had stayed in Simcoe after Scott and I parted. But I
now felt a need to be closer to Milton, who was eighty-
seven, and my sister Edna, who was eighty-five. Both of
them were living in Waterloo." And so Vera made the
decision to sell her beloved Oak Street home and return
to Waterloo Region, where she had been born and
raised. She purchased a condominium at the Eastwood
Complex, which had been founded by Milton, a gener-
ous philanthropist.

Her stay at Eastwood was brief, as health concerns
began to impact Vera's independence. Macular degen-
eration was making it difficult for her to drive, and she
was forced to give up her condo. A move in 2007 to the
upscale Chartwell Terrace on the Square, an assisted-
living complex in Waterloo, followed. Vera's time here
was relatively brief. Her sister Edna had recently relocated to Simcoe from Waterloo and had entered

Cedarwood Gardens Retirement and Nursing Facility. Milton's death in 2008 left her with no close family in Waterloo. There was no longer any reason for Vera to stay.

In 2010 she decided to move back to Simcoe. One of Cedarwood's assisted-living apartments would prove convenient for daily visits to Edna in the nursing-home division of the large complex. It was at Cedarwood that Vera took an intriguing telephone call.

57

Unexpected Recognition

Vera's caller was Dr. Max Blouw, the President of Wilfrid Laurier University (WLU) in Waterloo.

> *Dr. Blouw was calling me with a question that I frankly was unprepared for. He was asking me if I would accept an honorary doctoral degree – a DLitt from the university. It left me a bit at a loss for words at first. I was surprised, as none of my family had attended WLU. None of us really had any links with the university.*

Still, Vera was flattered, and she accepted the invitation.

Dr. Carol Duncan, of the university's Faculty of Religion and Culture, had been Vera's nominator. She gives the rationale behind her nomination: "I discovered *Polka Dot Door* as an elementary school–aged child and I loved it – the characters, the fun, and the Polkaroo of course." Later, as an academic, Dr. Duncan had admired other qualities of the long-running children's program – its creativity and the good learning principles behind it. "*Polka Dot Door* was everything I thought a children's learning experience on television should be."[94]

When Dr. Duncan, now teaching at Wilfrid Laurier University in Waterloo, learned that former Waterloo Region resident Vera Good was the founding Executive Producer of *Polka Dot Door*, she felt there was a strong basis for Dr. Good to be nominated for an honorary degree. "So I put the nomination forward and it went through the various vetting steps."

One of those steps was contacting Vera's nephew Dr. James Good to gauge his reaction to the honour and ask how he felt his aunt would respond. Jim thought Vera would be delighted. He notified Vera that she might receive a call in the coming days, but did not go into great detail of its nature. And so in late January 2010, when Dr. Blouw made his call to Vera, she had been "prepped" ahead of time. And she was pleased to accept the invitation.

Over the next months leading to the June 7, 2010 convocation, where she would be presented with her degree, Vera worked on her speech. Low vision precluded her being able to refer to any notes during her address to graduates, so she would need to rely on her prodigious memory. Jim Good would be on hand nearby to prompt if his services were needed.

During this time, I paid a visit to Vera to congratulate her on the honour. "Are you nervous at all, Vera?" I asked. "Are you worried that you'll forget your speech?" "I better not," she answered. "Every night before I go to bed, I say the entire speech to myself. I'm quite sure I'll have it down pat."

In the weeks before the convocation, Vera learned that she would have her degree conferred on the final day of Wilfrid Laurier's 2010 Spring Convocation exercises, held at the university's massive athletic complex. Dr. Good would be in distinguished company in receiving her honour. Writers Wayson Choi and Lawrence Hill, singer and First Nations activist Buffy St. Marie, and philanthropist Francis Pang were also being recognized with honorary degrees.

Vera admits to having "some nerves" as she took her place in the procession moving towards the convocation stage, entering on the arm of her nephew Jim. Both would sit with other honoured guests on the podium. After opening remarks were delivered to the graduates and their families, Vera rose to deliver her address. Over the next several minutes her delivery proved flawless and drew compliments from the large audience.

Sitting at the end of a row of graduates, I was as interested in the reaction that I observed from the graduating students as I was in Vera's words. As she confidently executed her speech, the student body listened intently. At one point near the conclusion of Vera's address, a graduate sitting beside me turned to another and whispered: "Do you realize she doesn't have any notes? She's memorized the entire speech and she hasn't made a mistake. Wow!" Later, Vera qualified that observation: "I actually did stop for just a second to collect my thoughts. Jim was just ready in the wings to feed me the word I needed. But then I picked it up myself."

The convocation crowd rose as one to give Dr. Vera Good a standing ovation. In thinking back to that memorable occasion, she says: "I was in the moment; I was confident and in control."

PART TEN

Vera the Centenarian

(2010–2017)

58
Trouble Comes to Call

Into her centenary year, Vera's mind remained
sharp, with her memory outstanding. Unlike many
seniors whose recollections extend back to childhood
but whose short-term memory is significantly impaired,
Vera's cognitive abilities remained strong in both past
and present time. As she approached her 100th year, it
was her body that was showing her age.

Unable now to use her computer, even with its en-
larged font size, she kept her faculties sharp by listening
to books on tape. Never much of a television watcher
for entertainment, she kept an ear open for news in
Canada, in the United States, where she had lived for a
number of years, and in the world beyond.

With her mobility diminishing, Vera accepted
that she would need to relocate to a facility with more
nursing care. In 2012, she took up residence in the large
Norview Lodge long-term care complex in Simcoe.
Close to family members and receiving the care she

now needed, Vera was content. But dark clouds were gathering in the months leading up to her birthday.

Despite the usual aches and pains – she was, after all, turning 100 on November 15, 2015 – Vera customarily faced each day in good health. But as the fall came, she was feeling poorly. The doctor diagnosed digestive issues and prescribed treatment. Still, her condition worsened and she was hospitalized.

In hospital, Vera suffered two heart attacks. "We were sure that we were going to lose her," recalls her niece Mary Beth Smith. Eventually Vera did recover enough to return to Norview, but, says Mary Beth, "she was a shadow of her former self and needed a lift to get out of bed and into her chair." As worrisome to the family was Vera's psychological state. Mary Beth remembers that "she was miserable and questioned me on a daily basis as to why everyone was working so hard to keep her alive." Mary Beth was with Vera during a telephone conversation between her aunt and Vera's younger brother Harold:

> *He encouraged her to let go and assured her that we would all be okay without her. He told her what a wonderful sister she had always been to him and*

*how much everyone in our family had always ap-
preciated her giving spirit. He said that her work
was done and it was time to quit fighting and just
let go.*

It was during this conversation that Mary Beth
recognized a transformation occurring in Vera. "It was
interesting to watch her reaction as he spoke. I knew
then and there deep down she had no intention of let-
ting go and she had every intention of a full recovery."

After this conversation, a spark began to glim-
mer once again in Vera. She worked daily with Personal
Support Worker Cindy Gaetz and began doing exercises to strengthen her muscles. Vera also began once
more to take an interest in the world outside her walls.
Her television was on, permanently settled on the CNN
News station, and she requested her books on tape to
while away the hours.

In March of 2016, Vera took a telephone call
that seemed to catch her interest, too. That caller was
me, and I had a proposal that I asked Vera to consider.
Looking for a subject for a new biography that I hoped
to write, my sights had landed on Vera. I was aware that
she had the honour of having been the first woman in
Ontario to be appointed an Inspector of Schools and
carried the distinction of being the conceptual heart of
Polka Dot Door, but I knew little more about her. Still, a
certain instinct persuaded me to pursue the goal.

And so in March of 2016, I travelled to Simcoe

to speak more fully about what I hoped would be a lengthy relationship – biographer interviewing subject. Vera's modest reply to my invitation would prove to be an ironic one. "I'm willing, but I don't think I've done anything to make my life very interesting!" Some coaxing convinced the diminutive centenarian that indeed her life was a shining one. And so she and I began our journey together.

Beginning on a farm on Woolwich Township, Waterloo County, it followed a winding path from factory work, then teaching, to a front-row seat in the theatre of India's independence. The journey continued on to undergraduate and graduate university degrees, to attaining the highest level of education administration in the province of Ontario. It saw her in a pioneering role in early educational television and reached an apex with scholarly and community recognition.

Along the way, too, Vera Good found love – and experienced loss.

59
Starting on a New Journey

Having passed her 101st birthday on November 13, 2016, Vera remains tuned in to her world. Her large-screen television is invariably on when visitors arrive. But no game shows and celebrity voyeurism for this lady: her dial is permanently set to the news channel. Vera remains as she has always been, a citizen of the world.

On one wall hang the visual memories of a life well lived: Vera flanked by two faculty members of Wilfrid Laurier University on the occasion of her honorary Doctorate of Letters (DLitt) degree. Another recognizes her as a Gemini Award winner for her work as Executive Producer of *Polka Dot Door*.

Sharing shelf space with various other memorabilia is the Polkaroo himself. When I borrowed the rascally 'Roo for a two-week "field trip," Vera reports that nursing and cleaning staff missed him. "They were glad when he returned," she chuckles. She gives the polka-dot-clad "stuffy" a fond hug. It's clear Vera herself welcomes him back home.

At the end of our journey together, chronicling ten decades of an exceptional life, I ask Vera to reflect on her greatest memories. Not surprisingly, given her innate modesty, she bypasses her achievements in the fields of education and educational television for memories of a happy and secure childhood, growing up on a small farm.

> *My fondest memories take place at our farm home. I remember like it was only yesterday, playing dolls with my sisters in the little playhouse which our mother created for us. And the tea parties she served to us. I remember my sisters and me playing in the woods across the road from our house, picking wildflowers to take home to Mother, hiding in the hay mow at the top of our barn.*

She calls them "carefree days." "We remained ignorant of the troubles of the world around us: the wounded men who came home from the First World War; the families who mourned family members who didn't come home at all." Vera's recollections also dance over solitary time – usually in nature. "My favourite place to sit and think was on an old stump in our orchard." It was here that the young Vera pondered: "What am I going to be? What am I going to do with my life?"

Work and accomplishment also rise to the top of Vera's long journey back in time. Not unexpectedly, memories of work do not necessarily include those jobs that included a paycheque. "I remember the satisfied feeling as my sisters and I hoed a row of potatoes in our garden. Dad was always there encouraging us: 'Just one more row and we're all done, girls.'"

Snippets of her two years' teaching at Riverbank School eclipse later, more prestigious assignments.

> *These were the days when kids went out for recess all on their own – there was no teacher on yard duty needing to supervise them. Warm-weather times were the best, with baseball games and marbles and girls skipping. I'd go outside to tell the kids that recess was over and they'd beg: "Just five minutes more, Miss Good, just five more minutes."*

Memories of India surface, too, but few are warm and glowing. "We knew we were in India to help, but it was difficult to see the good that we were doing when there was so much hatred and killing going on." Recalling the conditions in the Indian refugee camps also trumps positive memories of three years living in a country that Vera calls "stunningly beautiful." But "to see people – especially the little children – living this way… And there was so little that we could do."

Of her achievements in education, Vera saves her warmest memories for teaching children to read. "To

watch their minds opening up to books was so rewarding. I wish I had been able to spend more time in the
classroom."

And of her decade as a pioneer of educational
television, Vera has mixed emotions.

> *Because we had no feedback from our audience like
> teachers had, it was hard to really celebrate our
> work. And because, especially in the beginning, we
> were working blind, with nothing on which we
> could model our work, it was frustrating. It was
> almost impossible to get the same sort of satisfaction
> that teaching brought.*

Born as World War I was raging on the battlefields and trenches of Europe, Vera Good has lived to
see unparalleled changes in her world. And with an
open heart and exploring mind, she has embraced them.
With her love of learning still intact, she looks at each
new day as an adventure.

Bibliography

"About Goshen College." Goshen College. https://www.goshen.edu. Accessed Feb. 3, 2017.

"About Northwestern: History." Northwestern University. http://www.northwestern.edu.

"About OISE." Ontario Institute for Studies in Education. http://www.oise.utoronto.ca/oise/About_OISE/History_Facts.html.

"Bearinger Public School." Mennonite Archival Image Database. https://archives.mhsc.ca/bearinger-public-school-waterloo-ontario.

"Bearinger School." Region of Waterloo Public Building Inventory. Educational Buildings – Part 2. Region of Waterloo, n.d. http://www.regionofwaterloo.ca/en/discoveringTheRegion/resources/Public_Building_Inventory_Part_2_-_Educational_Buildings.pdf.

Bender, Harold S., and Elmer Neufeld. "Mennonite Central Committee (International)." 1987. *Global Anabaptist Mennonite Encyclopedia Online*. http://gameo.org. Accessed March 23, 2017.

Bérci, Margaret E. Review of *From Hope to Harris: The Reshaping of Ontario's Schools*, by R. Douglas Gidney. *Canadian Social Studies* 38, no. 2 (Winter 2004). https://sites.educ.ualberta.ca/css/Css_38_2/BRhope_to_harris.htm.

Bereday, G.Z., and J.A. Lauwerys, eds. *The Gifted Child*. Yearbook of Education 1962. London: Evans Bros., 1962.

"A Brief History of Gifted and Talented Education." National Association for Gifted Children. http://www.nagc.org/resources-publications/resources/gifted-education-us/brief-history-gifted-and-talented-education.

Davis, William G. "Speech of Education Minister William Davis." Ontario Legislature, June 2, 1965. *Hansard* 3583–3584.

"Discovery Learning (Bruner)." Learning Theories.com. https://www.learning-theories.com/discovery-learning-bruner.html.

Doucette, Travis. "An Interview with Dr. Vera Good," Aug. 13, 2013. YouTube. https://www.youtube.com/watch?v=paGRH4DAPs4.

Eby, Ezra E. *From Pennsylvania to Waterloo: A Biographical History of Waterloo Township. http://ebybook.region.waterloo.on.ca. Originally published Berlin, ON: 1895–96*.

"Egerton Ryerson 1803–1882." Ryerson University Library and Archives, Archives and Special Collections. https:library-ryerson.ca/asc/archives/Ryerson-history/Ryerson-bio.

"Egerton Ryerson Stream." Victoria College, University of Toronto. http://www.vic.utoronto.ca.

Epp-Tiessen, Esther. "Mennonite Central Committee Canada." June 2015. *Global Anabaptist Mennonite Encyclopedia Online.* http://gameo.org. Accessed March 27, 2017.

Fretz, Joseph C., and Sam Steiner. "Martin Mennonite Meetinghouse (Waterloo, Ontario, Canada)." June 1997. *Global Anabaptist Mennonite Encyclopedia Online.* http://gameo.org. Accessed March 23, 2017.

Fretz, Joseph C., and Sam Steiner. "Mennonite Conference of Ontario and Quebec." 1990. *Global Anabaptist Mennonite Encyclopedia Online.* http://gameo.org. Accessed March 27, 2017.

"Gandhi's First Act of Civil Disobedience." *This Day in History,* June 7 (1893). History Television, Corus Entertainment, 2017. http://www.history.com/this-day-in-history/gandhis-first-act-of-civil-disobedience.

Gelman, Susan. "Stratford (Normal School) Teachers College, 1908–1973." *Historical Studies in Education/Revue d'histoire de l'éducation* 14, no. 1 (2002): 113–20. http://historicalstudiesineducation.ca/index.php/edu_hse-rhe/article/view/1926/0ww.historical.

Gidney, R.D. "Ryerson, Egerton." *Dictionary of Canadian Biography.* Vol. 11. University of Toronto/Université Laval, 1982. Accessed July 22, 2017. http://www.biographi.ca/en/bio/ryerson_egerton_11E.html.

Good, M.R. *A Good Family Genealogy: A Detailed Record of the Descendants of Menno Good (1838–1919).* Breslau, ON, 1979.

Good, M.R. *A Martin Family Genealogy: A Detailed Record of the Descendants of Isaac D. Martin (1844–1931).* Waterloo, ON, 1968.

Good, Vera. *Our Family Odyssey … 1877–1977.* 1980.

Good, Vera. *Reflections.* 2005.

Good, Viola. " My Pilgrimage." In *Our Family Odyssey … 1877–1977,* by Vera Good. 1980.

Hall, Emmett, L.A. Dennis, et al. *Living and Learning: The Report of the Provincial Committee on Aims and Objectives of Education in the Schools of Ontario* (The Hall-Dennis Report). Ontario Ministry of Education, 1968. http://www.connexions.org/CxLibrary/Docs/CX5636-HallDennis.htm. Accessed March 22, 2017.

"Hey Ram Were Gandhi's Last Words Says Grandson." *Times of India,* Feb. 1, 2006. http://timesofindia.indiatimes.com/india/Hey-Ram-were-Gandhis-last-words-says-grandson/articleshow/1395570. cms.

Hodgetts, A.B. *Decisive Decades*. Toronto: Thomas Nelson and Sons, 1960.

Ide, T. Ranald. *The Transparent Blackboard: TVOntario: A Memoir*. Toronto: Lugus Press, 1994.

"Jerome Bruner." Sept. 2016. *Encyclopaedia Britannica*. https://www.britannica.com/biography/Jerome-Bruner.

J.L. "Discovery Learning (Bruner)." *Learning Theories*, Feb. 2, 2017. https://www.learning-theories.com/discovery-learning-bruner.html.

"John Forsyth (1850–1916)." Waterloo Region Generations. http://generations.regionofwaterloo.ca/getperson.php?personID=I97975&tree=generations. *Accessed Feb. 14, 2017.*

Kessler, Karl. "Snider, Jonas (1858–1944)." 2006. *Global Anabaptist Mennonite Encyclopedia Online*. http://gameo.org. Accessed March 23, 2017.

Kitchen, Julian, and Diana Petrarca. "Teacher Preparation in Ontario: A History." In *Teaching and Learning* 8, no. 1 (2013/2014): 56–71. https://brock.scholarsportal.info/journals/teachingandlearning/home/article/viewFile/426/381.

Laycock, Samuel. "Trends in the Education of Gifted Children in Canada." In *The Gifted Child*, edited by George Z.F. Bereday and Joseph A. Lauwerys. Yearbook of Education 1962. London: Evans Bros., 1962.

Mountbatten, Lord Louis. Personal Report no. 17, Aug. 16, 1947. In "Indian Independence: Transfer of Power," Source 6. India Office Records, British Library. http://www.bl.uk/reshelp/findhelpregion/asia/india/indianindependence/transfer/transfer6/index.html.

"Martin Family." Waterloo Region Generations. http://generations.regionofwaterloo.ca/family groups.

McLeod, Saul A. "Bruner." 2008. Simply Psychology. https://www.simplypsychology.org/bruner/html.

Millar John, B.A. *The Education System of the Province of Ontario*. Toronto: Warnock and Sons, 1893.

Ontario College of Teachers. "Revised Regulations of Ontario." Vol. 3. 1980.

Ontario Department of Education. "Schools and Teachers in the Province of Ontario." 1965.

Ontario Ministry of Education. Toronto: Report of the Minister. Supervision Division. 1965, 1966.

Paetkau, Henry. "Conference of United Mennonite Churches in Ontario." 1990. *Global Anabaptist Mennonite Encyclopedia Online*. http://gameo.org. Accessed March 23, 2017.

P.T.I. "62 Years after His Death, Gandhi's Ashes Immersed off Durban." *The Tribune*, Jan. 31, 2010. http://www.tribuneindia.com/2010/20100131/main3.htm.

"Quit India Movement." HistoryDiscussion.Net, 2016. http://www.historydiscussion.net/history-of-india/-quit-india-movement/3194.

Ramesh, Randeep. "60 Years On, Gandhi's Ashes Laid to Rest." *The Guardian*, World News, Jan. 31, 2008. https://www.theguardian.com/world/2008/jan/31/india.international.

"Riverbank School." Region of Waterloo Public Buildings inventory_Pt 2, Educational Buildings pdf. http://www.waterlooregionmuseum.com.

Robarts, John P. "Statement by Premier John P. Robarts." Ontario Legislature, May 31, 1962. *Hansard*.

Roberts, J.M. "India's Independence." In *The Penguin History of the Twentieth Century*, 369–74. London: Penguin Books, 1999.

Robinson, Dean. *Hardly Normal, the Stratford Normal School and Stratford Teachers College 1908–1973*. Stratford, ON: Friends of the Stratford Normal School/Teachers' College Heritage, with support from the Stratford Perth Museum, 2011.

Robinson, Kyle, Matt Hendry, Kim Eyers, Lukas Rebl, and Kurt Bagg. "The Development of Special Education Programs in the Province of Ontario, 1950–2012." Paper submitted for the course Introduction to Teaching History, November 19, 2012.

Roes, Marion. "Erb Street Mennonite Church (Waterloo, Ontario, Canada)." July 2015. *Global Anabaptist Mennonite Encyclopedia Online*. http://gameo.org. Accessed March 23, 2017.

Rosen, Armin. "The Birth and Partition of a Nation: India's Independence Told in Photos." http://www.theatlantic.com/international/archive/2012/08.

Royal Commission on Education in Ontario Report. 1950.

Stanford, J.K. "Dak Bungalows." 1961. The Kipling Society. http://www.kiplingsociety.co.uk/rg_bungalows.htm.

Steiner, Sam. "Martin, Abraham W. (1834–1902)." July 2002. *Global Anabaptist Mennonite Encyclopedia Online*. http://gameo.org. Accessed March 23, 2017.

Steiner, Sam. "Mennonite Historical Society of Ontario." November 2010.

Global Anabaptist Mennonite Encyclopedia Online. http://gameo.org. Accessed March 27, 2017.

"Stratford Normal School." Canada's Historic Places. http://historicplaces. ca/en/rep-reg/place-lieu.aspx?id-8871.ss.

Stratford Normal School Historical Plaque-Ontario Historical Plaques Ontario. http://www.plaques.com/Plaques/plaque_Perth o5.html.

"Stratford YWCA." Stratford Tourism-Stratford History. https://www. visitstratford.ca/stratford-history.ca.

Student and Teacher Records. Archives of Ontario. http://www.archives. gov.on.ca/en/access/research-guide.216_student and teacher pdf.

Taylor, Kate. "A Teacher and TV Producer, Children Were Always at the Forefront of His Work." *Globe and Mail,* Jan. 27, 2012. https:// beta.theglobeandmail.com/news/national/a-teacher-and-tv- producer-children-were-always-at-the-forefront-of-his-work/ article543622/?ref=http://www.theglobeandmail.com&.

Terman, Lewis M. "Mental and Physical Traits of a Thousand Gifted Children." *Genetic Studies in Genius.* Vol. 1. Stanford, CA: Stanford University Press, 1925. http://hearth.library.cornell.edu/h/hearth/ browse/title/4216772.html.

Trick, David. "Robarts' Plan for Higher Education Goes Golden." *It's Not Academic* (blog), March 20, 2013. Higher Education Quality Council of Ontario (HEQCO). http://blog-en.heqco.ca/2013/03/.

Umble, John S. "Goshen College (Goshen, Indiana, USA)." 1956. *Global Anabaptist Mennonite Encyclopedia Online.* http://gameo.org. Re- trieved March 24, 2017.

Vance, Pat, Ruth Baumann, et al. *A Different Understanding: Learning Dis- abilities.* Toronto: OISE, 1981.

Virag, Sarah. "Feature from the Collections: Looking Back at the His- tory of the Normal School Building – Part Two." April 25, 2013. Ryerson University Library and Archives, Archives and Special Collections. https://library.ryerson.ca/asc/2013/04/feature-from- the-collections-looking-back-at-the-history-of-the-normal- school-building-part-two/.

Wenger, John C. "Old Order Mennonites." 2002. *Global Anabaptist Men- nonite Encyclopedia Online.* http://gameo.org. Accessed March 23, 2017.

Zachariah, Benjamin. "Gandhi, Non-Violence, and Independence." *History Review* 69 (March 2011). http://www.historytoday.com/archive/ history-review/issue-69-march-2011.

Zegarac, George. *Closing the Gap as the Overreaching Goal: Changing Special Educational Practices and Outcomes.* Toronto: Ontario Ministry of Education, 2008.

Endnotes

1   Wenger, "Old Order Mennonites"; Paetkau, "Conference of United Mennonite Churches in Ontario."

2   Steiner, "Martin, Abraham W. (1834–1902)."

3   M.R. Good, *A Martin Family Genealogy*; "Martin Family," Waterloo Region Generations.

4   M.R. Good, *A Martin Family Genealogy*. Documentation regarding Isaac's school board participation found in Records of Elmira School Board (1879), held in Rare Books of the Waterloo Region District School Board.

5   Unless another source is referenced, all direct quotations from Vera Good throughout this book come from interviews with the author conducted March 2016 through June 2017.

6   Ernie Ritz, interview with author, New Hamburg, July 18, 2016.

7   M.R. Good, *A Good Family Genealogy*.

8   Fretz and Steiner, "Martin Mennonite Meetinghouse (Waterloo, Ontario, Canada)."

9   Rick Cober Bauman, MCC Canada Executive Director, interview with author, March 8, 2017.

10 Laureen Harder-Gissing, email to author, March 21, 2014; Paul Tiessen, email to author, March 19, 2017; Mabel Hunsberger, email to author, March 20, 2017.

11 Kessler, "Snider, Jonas (1858–1944)"; Paetkau, "Conference of United Mennonite Churches in Ontario."

12 Roes, "Erb Street Mennonite Church (Waterloo, Ontario, Canada)."

13 Kessler, "Snider, Jonas (1858–1944)."

14 Barbara Draper, interview with author, March 17, 2017.

15 Church records, Erb Street Mennonite Church, Waterloo, ON.

16 "Bearinger Public School," Mennonite Archival Image Database; "Bearinger School," Region of Waterloo Public Building Inventory.

17 "John Forsyth (1850–1916)," Waterloo Region Generations.

18 Viola Good, "My Pilgrimage," 10.

19 R.N. Merritt was principal of Kitchener Collegiate and Vocational School (KCI) from 1921 to 1944.

20 Up until 1973, elementary teachers in Ontario's public schools needed only grade 13 and a year at teachers' college to be qualified to teach. Ontario College of Teachers, "Revised Regulations of Ontario," vol. 3,

reg. 269, p. 177, sec. 3c.

21 Viola Good, "My Pilgrimage," 10–14.

22 See Gelman, "Stratford (Normal School) Teachers College, 1908–1973"; Kitchen and Petrarca, "Teacher Preparation in Ontario: A History"; Virag, "Feature from the Collections: Looking Back at the History of the Normal School Building – Part Two."

23 "Egerton Ryerson 1803–1882," Ryerson University Library and Archives; Gidney, "Ryerson, Egerton."

24 "Stratford Normal School," Canada's Historic Places; Gelman, "Stratford (Normal School) Teachers College, 1908–1973."

25 "Stratford YWCA," Stratford Tourism-Stratford History.

26 "Riverbank School," Region of Waterloo Public Buildings inventory_Pt 2, Educational Buildings pdf.

27 Bender and Neufeld, "Mennonite Central Committee (International)."

28 Epp-Tiessen, "Mennonite Central Committee Canada."

29 Zachariah, "Gandhi, Non-Violence, and Independence."

30 "Quit India Movement," HistoryDiscussion.Net.

31 Hodgetts, *Decisive Decades*, 232–34.

32 Amritsar was the scene of a bloodbath in 1919, when British troops fired on unarmed demonstrators, killing 379.

33 Vera Good, letter to MCC, Akron, PA, Oct. 21, 1947. See also Roberts, "India's Independence."

34 Stanford, "Dak Bungalows."

35 Letter from Vera Good to J.N. Byler, Director of Relief, MCC, Akron, PA, Feb. 17, 1947.

36 Ibid., Oct. 21, 1947.

37 Letter from Vera Good to Vera Isaak, MCC, Akron, PA, Oct. 25, 1947.

38 Ibid., Sept. 24, 1948.

39 Ibid.

40 Vera Good, Activity Report to MCC, Akron, PA, July 1, 1948.

41 "Gandhi's First Act of Civil Disobedience," *This Day in History*, June 7 (1893).

42 Mountbatten, Personal Report no. 17, Aug. 16, 1947.

43 "Hey Ram Were Gandhi's Last Words Says Grandson," *Times of India*, Feb. 1, 2006.

44 Ramesh, "60 Years On, Gandhi's Ashes Laid to Rest," *The Guardian*, Jan. 31, 2008; P.T.I., "62 Years after His Death, Gandhi's Ashes Im-

mersed off Durban," *The Tribune*, Jan. 30, 2010.

45 Umble, "Goshen College (Goshen, Indiana, USA)."

46 "About Goshen College," Goshen College.

47 "About Northwestern: History," Northwestern University.

48 J.L., "Discovery Learning (Bruner)."

49 "Jerome Bruner," *Encyclopaedia Britannica*; McLeod, "Bruner."

50 When Vera began teaching in Etobicoke it was known as the Borough of Etobicoke. The Etobicoke Board of Education was officially formed in 1967 with the merger of the boards in the towns of Long Branch, New Toronto, and Mimico. For continuity, all references to Vera's employment in Etobicoke will be identified as "the Etobicoke Board of Education."

51 Records of employment held at the present-day Toronto District School Board.

52 "A Brief History of Gifted and Talented Education," National Association for Gifted Children.

53 Ibid.

54 Ibid.

55 Laycock, "Trends in the Education of Gifted Children in Canada," 227.

56 Robinson et al., "The Development of Special Education Programs in the Province of Ontario, 1950–1912," 32.

57 *Living and Learning: The Report of the Provincial Committee on Aims and Objectives of Education in the Schools of Ontario.* Commissioned by Ontario Minister of Education Bill Davis, it became known as the Hall-Dennis Report after the two co-chairs of the committee responsible for drafting it: Justice Emmet Hall (Supreme Court of Canada) and L.A. Dennis (a former school principal).

58 "The Truth Shall Make You Free," in Hall and Dennis, *Living and Learning*. Principles 1–3 are quoted from the United Nations Universal Declaration of Human Rights, Article 26.

59 Ibid.

60 The Ontario Institute for Studies in Education (OISE), one of the first Canadian institutions to offer graduate studies in education, opened in 1965. See "About OISE," Ontario Institute for Studies in Education.

61 "Statement by Premier John P. Robarts," Ontario Legislature, May 31, 1962.

62 Millar, *The Education System of the Province of Ontario*, 10.

63 Ontario teachers hoping to be granted their permanent teaching certificate would see an inspector at least once, probably twice, in their
first two years on the job.

64 Ontario Ministry of Education, Toronto: Report of the Minister,
Supervision Division, 10.

65 Ibid., 11.

66 Ontario Department of Education, "Schools and Teachers in the
Province of Ontario," part11-ms72, n.p.

67 Ibid.

68 Ontario Ministry of Education, Toronto: Report of the Minister
1965, Supervision Division, 10–14.

69 Ibid.

70 Ibid.

71 Ibid.

72 On May 21, 1965, Ontario's Minister of Education William Davis
announced the creation of a post-secondary college system separate
from that of the universities.

73 School Inspector (retired) Howard Parliament, interview with author,
Jan. 2017.

74 Ontario's Department of Education began closing small one- and
two-room elementary schools in the mid-1960s. Bearinger School,
which Vera attended as an elementary student, closed in 1960, and
Riverbank School, where she taught for two years, closed in 1963.

75 "Speech of Education Minister William Davis," Ontario Legislature,
June 2, 1965.

76 Educational television in Ontario underwent several name changes.
When Vera was conscripted in 1965, it was known as Educational
Television. By 1970, it had become Ontario Education Communications Authority (OECA), then finally TVOntario (TVO). For
continuity, all subsequent references will be to TVO.

77 "Speech of Education Minister William Davis," Ontario Legislature,
June 2, 1965.

78 Ide, *The Transparent Blackboard*, 3.

79 Ibid., 7.

80 Ibid., 52.

81 Ibid., 8.

82 Ibid., 35.

83 Ibid., 37.

84 Doucette, "An Interview with Dr. Vera Good," Aug. 13, 2013.

85   Ide, *The Transparent Blackboard*, 137.
86   Ibid., 37.
87   Louis Silcox, interview with author, July 3, 2016.
88   Ide, *The Transparent Blackboard*, 52–53.
89   Quoted in Taylor, "A Teacher and TV Producer, Children Were Always at the Forefront of His Work."
90   Ibid.
91   Babs Church, interview with author, Aug. 22, 2016.
92   Ran Ide, tribute at Vera Good's retirement from TVO, 1981. From the personal files of Vera Good.
93   Milton R. Good was inducted into the Waterloo Country Hall of Fame in 1996.
94   Dr. Carol Duncan, interview with author, June 21, 2016.

Manufactured by Amazon.ca
Bolton, ON

26209546R00146